Wallcoverings: Paneling, Painting, and Papering

Robert Scharff

Ideals Publishing Corp.
Milwaukee, Wisconsin

Table of Contents

ISBN 0-8249-6123-4

Copyright © 1982 by Ideals Publishing Corporation

Published by Ideals Publishing Corporation
11315 Watertown Plank Road
Milwaukee, Wisconsin 53226

Editor, David Schansberg

Cover design by David Schansberg. Materials courtesy of Elm Grove Ace Hardware.

Cover photo by Jerry Koser

⌂ SUCCESSFUL
HOME IMPROVEMENT SERIES

Bathroom Planning and Remodeling
Kitchen Planning and Remodeling
Space Saving Shelves and Built-ins
Finishing Off Additional Rooms
Finding and Fixing the Older Home
Money Saving Home Repair Guide
Homeowner's Guide to Tools
Homeowner's Guide to Electrical Wiring
Homeowner's Guide to Plumbing
Homeowner's Guide to Roofing and Siding
Homeowner's Guide to Fireplaces
Home Plans for the '80s
Planning and Building Home Additions
Homeowner's Guide to Concrete and Masonry
Homeowner's Guide to Landscaping
Homeowner's Guide to Swimming Pools
Homeowner's Guide to Fastening Anything
Planning and Building Vacation Homes
Homeowner's Guide to Floors and Staircases
Home Appliance Repair Guide
Homeowner's Guide to Wood Refinishing
Children's Rooms and Play Areas
Wallcoverings: Paneling, Painting, and Papering
Money Saving Natural Energy Systems
How to Build Your Own Home

Color and Your Walls

When you are covering your walls, whether it be with paneling, paint, or wallcovering, color must be a consideration. Judge both by your likes and dislikes and by the effect the color will have on the room. Remember that you must live with your choice.

Paneling blends in well with nearly any existing color scheme and adapts readily to new ones. Although we think of paneling as coming only in the wood tones of browns, golds, and grays, many other colors and patterns are available. Some of these are printed directly on the boards; others are in the form of overlays that are bonded to the panels. Paneling can also simulate the color and texture of other natural materials such as brick and stone. The main advantages of paneling are that it covers wall defects and can be installed by itself in new construction; that is, it can be directly attached to studs without the need for a backing material.

Paint can be custom mixed to match any color imaginable. White, alone, comes in 25 or more types. Paint not only offers the most colors, but it is also the easiest and least expensive method of decorating walls. Of course, paint cannot cover major wall defects, but the textured variety can minimize or camouflage minor flaws.

Wallcoverings fall midway between paneling and paint in terms of cost and installation ease. Wallcoverings combine the colors of paint and the textures of paneling with a multitude of patterns of their own. They can be applied over most surfaces and come in a wide range of materials.

Properties of Color

Whether or not we are conscious of it, color plays a significant role in many of our daily decisions. It is color that makes you choose the green tie instead of the purple one, or leads you to pick up a full-color magazine rather than its black and white competitor. We have all been exposed to the influence of color in such things as television, photographs, and brightly colored product packaging designed to catch the eye of the consumer.

When we see colors, our eyes are picking up various lengths of light waves that are reflecting off the objects around us. These waves are best represented by the colors that make up a rainbow: red, orange, yellow, green, blue, indigo, and violet. To refer to them we can use the term chromatic colors.

What about white, black, and gray? These are more properly called neutrals because they will blend in with any of the chromatic colors. White is the reflection of all colors. If you have ever used a prism, you have seen how white light can be broken down into all of the rainbow colors. White will make any area look bigger and brighter. Along with pure white, there are the off-whites. Off-whites have a small amount of some chromatic color added to them. Like the chromatic colors, off-whites can affect the apparent temperature of a room—a concept that will be discussed later. On the other hand, black absorbs all the light waves coming into it and reflects none. Black is generally a poor choice for any large scale use because its nonreflective property

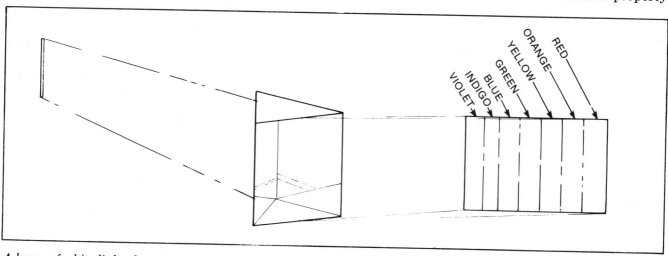

A beam of white light shot through a prism produces a rainbow spectrum.

hinders room lighting. Gray, a combination of white and black, evenly reflects and absorbs light. Brown is often included under the neutrals because it is the color of wood, a prominent material in cabinetry and furniture. An entire color scheme planned around one of these neutrals tends to be quite dull, but they are effective accents when combined with one or more colors.

The Color Wheel   The color wheel is one of the best tools you can use to help you understand the relationships between colors. Any good art instruction book should have one included, or you can ask at your local home center if they have one you can look at. The color wheel has three levels with which you should become familiar: primary, secondary, and tertiary colors.

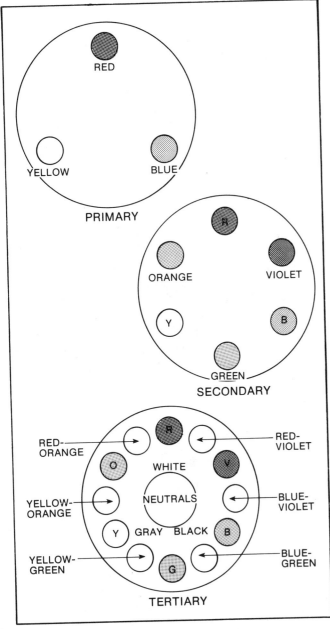

The three levels of color on the color wheel.

Primary colors are the base colors. These three colors—red, blue, and yellow—cannot be mixed from any other colors. They serve as the building blocks for all the rest of the colors on the wheel. Red can be overwhelming when used as a main room color. Blue is a peaceful, tranquil color. It is useful in rooms where rest and relaxation is the prime concern. Yellow can brighten up any area and may bring to mind sunflowers and warm summer days.

The secondary colors of violet, green, and orange are mixed from equal amounts of two primary colors. They are located between their respective primary colors on the color wheel. Violet and orange, like red, are best used as accent colors. As dominant room colors, they can be too strong. Green is a comfortable color, though it has been somewhat overused.

Combine equal amounts of a primary and a secondary color and the result is a tertiary color. In naming, the primary color is named first, followed by the name of the secondary color: red-orange, red-violet, blue-violet, blue-green, yellow-green, and yellow-orange.

Color Terms   When you are working with or reading about color, there are several terms you should understand: hue, value, and intensity. Although they are frequently interchanged in conversation, they actually refer to three very different things.

The hue of a color is merely another name for the color itself. Red, green, and blue are all hues. The degree of lightness or darkness of a color is its value. On a scale from one to ten, white is one and black is ten. Light values, colors to which white has been added, are called tints. Shades are the darker values to which black has been added. Intensity is the brightness or dullness of a color. All pure colors are bright; dull ones have gray mixed in. The more gray that is added, the duller the color becomes. If someone says the color has a tinge of gray, it means a very small amount has been added.

When decorating, you will be interested in how these concepts relate to the overall color scheme. If you want to make the most out of a bright color, play it up by using it with a dull one. Two equally bright colors, side by side, tend to dull each other. The same principle applies when you are working with shades and tints. A shade and a tint will always be more effective than two like values combined.

Color Schemes   The wall material you choose (unless it is a solid color) as well as the room you are decorating will center around one of three color schemes: monochromatic, complementary, or analogous. Since we have already discussed the workings of the color wheel, these schemes will be much easier to understand.

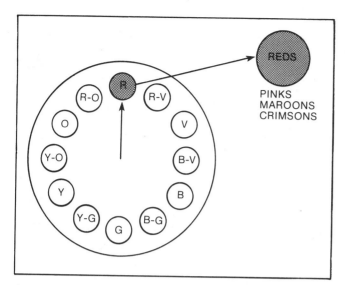

Sample of a monochromatic color scheme centering on red.

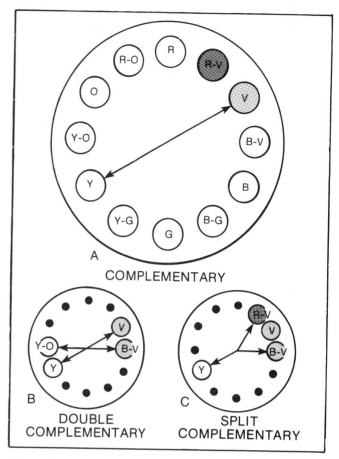

A complementary color scheme and its variations.

Monochromatic color schemes utilize different values of the same color; in other words, you pick the pure color of your choice and then lighten and/or darken it. For example, if you chose red, the values could range from the palest pinks to the deepest maroons and crimsons. Flocked damask-patterned wallcoverings often employ such a color scheme. In some respects, the wood tones in paneling can also be seen as monochromatic. Total monochromatic color schemes, however, can be rather boring—too much of one thing. To add variety, employ one or more of the neutrals.

More daring are the complementary color schemes that combine two colors which are opposite each other on the color wheel. Most of these pairings, such as yellow and violet, blue and orange, and red-violet and yellow-green, will sound strange to you and rightly so. Complementary color schemes are often employed for their shock value. If they are a bit too shocking for you, try having one color dominate, using the complement as an accent. You also can do one wall in a complementary-colored graphic design.

There are two variations on the basic complementary scheme that you should consider. Double complementary schemes are made up of four colors in all—two colors that are side by side on the wheel and their respective complements. You could try, for example, yellow and yellow-orange and their respective complements of violet and blue-violet. A split complementary color scheme takes a color plus the colors on either side of the complement. So instead of matching yellow with violet, you would use red-violet and blue-violet.

The last combination, the analogous scheme, mixes two or three colors that are adjacent to each other on the color wheel. Generally, these combina-

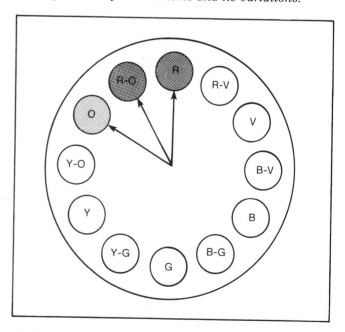

Analogous color schemes include colors directly alongside one another on the color wheel.

tions stay within one color temperature range such as red, red-orange, and orange in the warm sector or blue, blue-green, and green in the cool sector. Analogous schemes are very common in splashy and all-over petite florals.

The Effects of Color

Color greatly influences how a room looks and how you feel while in the room. Although these effects are in a sense psychological, they should still be given careful consideration.

Temperature   As mentioned when discussing the analogous color scheme, the color wheel is divided into warm and cool colors. The warm, or sunshine, colors are the reds, yellows, and oranges. The cool colors, often called the dusk or sea colors, are the violets, blues, and greens. Off-whites affect the temperature less than, but in the same way as, the chromatic color that has been added to them.

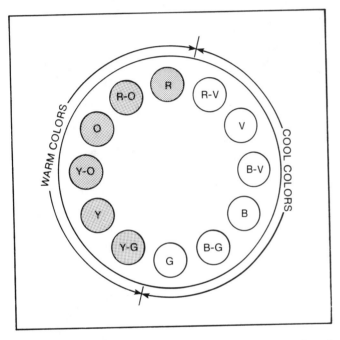

The color wheel can be subdivided into warm and cool colors.

Depending on which side of the color wheel you use, you can create certain temperature effects in a room. However, there are certain things you should consider. If the kitchen, for instance, has a sunny western or southern exposure, using bright yellows or oranges in the room would be unbearable. The heat of the sun combined with the steam from cooking and the warmth of the walls would have you melting in no time at all. Instead, use blues or greens that will counteract the heat. Cool colors cannot replace an air conditioner, but they can help. The same is true for the other rooms in the house. If your bedroom is in a chilly section of the house, warm it up with luxuriously rich reds, crimsons, and golds. Paneling, though a neutral, tends more to warm a room than to cool it. This is somewhat due to the image of wood as a warm and comforting material.

Size   Besides affecting the temperature of a room, color also creates illusions of size. Warm colors make the walls of a room advance, making the overall room seem smaller. To make a room appear larger, use cool colors. Values of colors also affect size. Tints will increase the visual size of a room, whereas shades of a color will diminish it. To make a room seem as large as possible, pick the palest tint of a cool color.

If you are redoing your ceiling as well, color can produce an illusion of height. A light color on the ceiling will make it appear higher. Use a dark color, and the ceiling will seem to drop lower. When working with a dark colored ceiling, however, the lighting in the room will have to be increased in order to compensate for the fact that dark colors do not reflect light as well as light colors do.

Working with Color   When you pick the color for your walls, you should take into consideration the surrounding furnishings and floor covering. Also take note of the colors used in rooms adjacent to the one in which you are working. Colors should continue or carry over from one room into the next. Sharp breaks in color have a way of making your overall decorating scheme look like a patchwork quilt. Pipes and other obstructions should be boxed in or painted in a color matching the walls. This will draw them into the background and make them less noticeable.

The best thing to do is to get samples of different wall materials at a home center, take them home, and put them up against your furniture, draperies, and flooring. Do not forget to consider lighting as well. Fluorescent tube fixtures play up the cool colors while dulling the warm ones. The reverse is true of incandescent bulbs. Sunlight can have an entirely different effect. Avoid trying to judge the colors solely by the way they look in the store. Seeing the colors and samples at home will give them an entirely new perspective.

Before taking a look at the various methods of applying color and decorative beauty to the rooms of your home or apartment, let us define the two basic types of wall construction—dry wall and lath-and-plaster. Though lath-and-plaster finish is still employed to a very limited degree in home construction, the use of dry wall materials is the most popular today. Dry wall finish, as the name implies, is a material that requires little, if any, water for application. A term usually employed to refer to dry wall construction materials is paneling. This can include plywood, hardboard, gypsum wallboard, or similar sheet material, as well as solid wood paneling in various thicknesses and forms.

Preparing to Paint Your Walls

One of the easier and less expensive ways to redo your walls is to paint them. Painting does require skill, but one of the main prerequisites is patience. If you take your time and avoid shortcuts, you can produce a professional-looking job. Paint allows you to be creative with colors, designs, and combinations. You do not need artistic talent to paint walls. What you do need is a critical eye. Take the extra time to properly prepare the wall and to avoid brush marks. Interior painting jobs are judged on neatness and smoothness, not speed. Try to think of painting as a challenge rather than merely a job that has to be done. A positive attitude can make a definite difference in the quality of work.

Methods of Applying Paint

To do a good job with a minimum of trouble, choose the right tools and learn how to handle them properly. When you are painting walls, you have a choice among three tools: a roller, a brush, and a spray gun. Which one you choose will depend on the job at hand and also somewhat on your personal preferences.

Using Rollers   The use of a roller is the quickest and most popular method of applying paint to walls. It has been estimated that this comparatively new painting tool is today being used to apply over 90 percent of all interior wall and ceiling paint.

Modern paint rollers are available in various sizes and with handles of different lengths. Many are built so that extensions can be screwed into their handles. This makes it possible to paint ceilings or stairwells as high as 12 feet while standing on the floor. Rollers are available in a variety of widths—from 2 to 36 inches—suitable for use on different size areas. For walls and ceilings, the best size roller for the amateur is the 7- or 9-inch model. For finished woodwork, doors, and trim, the best choice is the 3-inch model. There are smaller sizes available to cut in corners and for use on window frames and moldings. There are even doughnut-shaped rollers that will coat both sides of a corner at the same time. To help you paint a wall without getting the paint on the ceiling, there are special edging rollers, too.

Most paint trays are designed for use with a roller up to 9 inches wide. Roller frames can have a com-

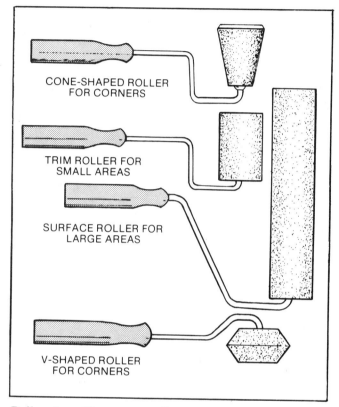

Roller size will vary according to the job.

CONE-SHAPED ROLLER FOR CORNERS

TRIM ROLLER FOR SMALL AREAS

SURFACE ROLLER FOR LARGE AREAS

V-SHAPED ROLLER FOR CORNERS

pression-type cage, or the roller cover can be held on with an end cap held by a wing nut. Compression frames permit easier and faster roller cover mounting or removal.

The fabric on the roller cover should conform to the type of paint to be applied. Lamb's wool rollers are excellent with oil-base paints, but they should not be used with water-thinned latex paints. Water softens and swells rayon and lamb's wool. These roller fabrics lose their resilience, and the fibers mat together when used in latex paints. Oil or alkyd paints and varnishes are usually thinned with mineral spirits or turpentine. Roller fabrics of most types are not affected by these thinners.

Walls can be made uniquely attractive by using a special roller to stipple a contrasting color over another one. Stippling rollers come in a wide assortment of design-producing sleeves. With these rollers, however, a different rolling technique must be used. The roll should be started at the left-hand side of the wall at the ceiling line, and the roller drawn evenly in a straight line to the floor. The second stroke should not overlap, but simply fit against the edge of the first.

Another factor to consider when choosing a roller is the length of the nap or pile. This can range from 1/16 to 1½ inches. A handy rule to remember is the smoother the surface, the shorter the nap; the rougher the surface, the longer the nap. Use short-napped rollers, usually ¼ inch, for most walls, ceilings, woodwork, and smooth concrete. The longer naps are for rough masonry, brick, stucco, and other irregular surfaces.

Before applying the paint with a roller, first cut in the edges of the wall and hard-to-reach areas with a brush or with an edging roller, taking care not to get paint on the ceiling or the adjacent wall. Some roller models have a roll that may be filled with paint, which soaks through a perforated backing into the pile cover. However, most rollers used by amateurs are manually loaded from a tilted pan which usually has a corrugated bottom. Make sure you get a heavy-gauge aluminum tray that can be securely anchored to a stepladder for painting the upper wall and ceiling areas. Before paint is poured into the roller tray, it should be thoroughly mixed in the can to assure even pigment distribution. The tray should be propped so that about two-thirds of the bottom is covered with paint.

Next, dip the roller into the tray. Dip it into the edge of the paint, rolling the tool back and forth over the slanting corrugated section of the tray to distribute the paint evenly over the entire surface of the roller and to remove excess paint. If the roller drips when lifted from the tray, it is overloaded. The excess should be wiped off on the dry side of the tilted tray before you begin your stroke.

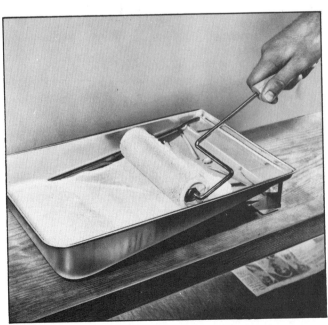

Roll out the paint on the corrugated tray bottom.

Apply even pressure when rolling paint on a surface. Even if the general direction of the painting may be downward, make your first stroke upward to avoid dripping. Work up and down first, doing about three strips; then work the roller horizontally to assure even coverage. As you progress, always start in a dry area and roll toward one just painted, blending in the laps.

Apply paint with an up-and-down motion, then roll horizontally or diagonally to fill in the gaps. Try to choose a paint tray that can be secured to the ladder.

When finished painting the walls, clean the roller as soon as possible. First, roll out any excess paint on a newspaper. Place heavy cardboard underneath so none bleeds through to the surface below. Then remove the roller cover or the roller itself (if it is the attached type) from the handle. Wash the roller or cover in solvent. (For rollers used with latex paint, use warm, sudsy water.) Work the nap between your fingers to loosen trapped paint. Wash in warm soapy water and rinse. Squeeze excess moisture out of the cover and dry by rubbing it on a clean cloth or by patting it between paper towels. Rollers can also be rolled on newspaper. After it has dried, wrap the cover or roller in aluminum foil.

The paint tray should also be cleaned after each use. For latex or other water-based paints, line the tray with aluminum foil to make the cleanup task easier.

Using a Brush While brushes are not used as much to paint walls as they once were, they still are the most effective way of painting around windows and doors, as well as applying paint to intricate trim. A brush is also handy for touch-up work.

For applying paint to trim, a 2- to 3-inch brush is generally used. Some painters find that an angular-cut brush helps to do a cleaner, neater job on sash or narrow trim and makes cutting in easier. For

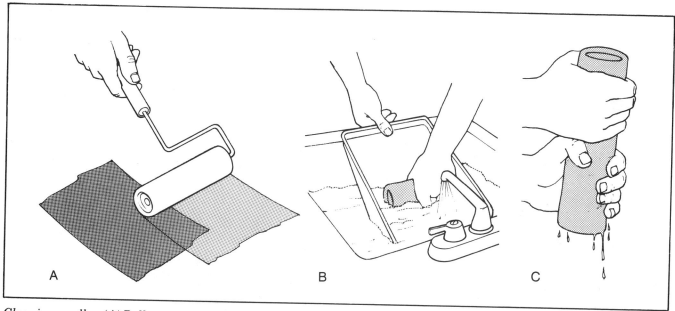

Cleaning a roller: (A) Roll out excess paint on newspaper, (B) wash the roller, and (C) wring out water.

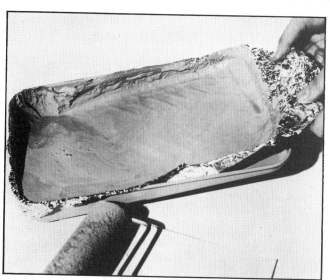

Lining the paint tray will make cleanup easier.

Brush quality determines painting ease, plus the quality of the finished job. A good brush holds more paint, controls dripping and spattering, and applies paint more smoothly to minimize brush marks. It is best to buy the highest quality brush you can afford.

larger surfaces, a 3½- to 6-inch brush may be employed. Brush prices vary considerably; the greatest difference between one brush and another lies in the bristle stock, which may be made from either natural or synthetic sources. Natural bristle brushes are made with hog hair. This type of brush was originally recommended for applying oil-base paints, varnishes, lacquers, and other finishes, because natural fibers resist strong solvents.

Synthetic bristle brushes are made from a synthetic fiber, usually nylon. Today's nylon brushes are recommended for both latex (water-soluble) and oil-base paints, because this tough synthetic fiber absorbs less water than natural bristles do, while also resisting most strong paint and lacquer solvents. In addition, nylon bristles are easier to clean than natural bristles.

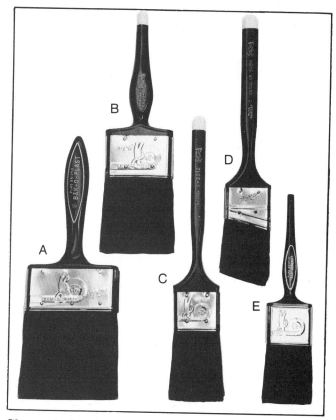

Choose the brush size that fits your needs: (A) 4-inch wall brush, (B) 3-inch enameling brush, (C) 2-inch trim brush, (D) 2-inch beveled sash brush, and (E) 2-inch varnish brush.

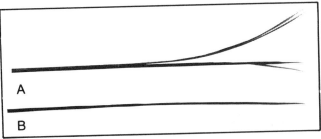

(A) Flagged and (B) tapered bristle ends provide for smooth paint flow.

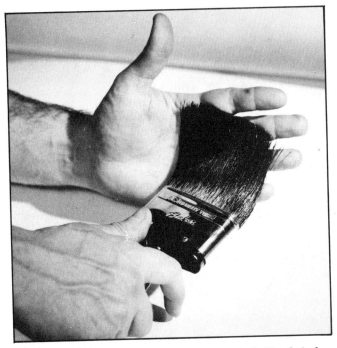

One way to tell a good brush is by its feel. The bristles should be full and bouncy.

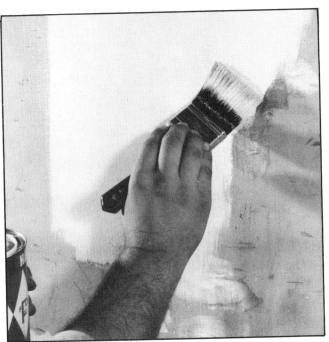

The proper method of holding a brush. Always paint using the flat side of the brush.

When applying paint to a wall or trim, remember that proper brushing helps bond the material to the work surface; therefore, it is very important that you learn the proper technique from the beginning. Hold the brush by gripping the wide part of the handle between your fingertips near the metal ferrule. The rest of the handle should be held between your thumb and forefinger, as you would grip a pencil. This is the best way to hold the brush except when working overhead. In this case wrap your hand around the handle with the thumb resting against the handle's inside curve. Use long, steady strokes and moderate, even pressure; excessive pressure or stuffing the brush into corners and cracks may damage the bristles. Even when painting a narrow strip, always use the flat side of the brush. Painting with the edge of the brush makes it divide into clumps.

Always work toward the wet edge of the previously painted area, making sure not to try to cover too large a surface with each brushload. When loading the brush with paint, do not dip more than half the bristle length into the paint. Tap the bristle tips lightly against the inside rim of the can to remove excess. Never wipe the brush edgewise across the rim. This removes more paint than necessary, causes the brush to separate or finger, and causes tiny bubbles that make it hard to get a smooth job. When carrying a brush loaded with paint, keep the bristle side down. This will prevent paint from running into the ferrule where it will cake and be hard to remove.

Dip only half the bristle length into the paint can.

Once you are finished using a brush, clean it immediately, being certain to use the thinner or special brush cleaner recommended by your paint or hardware store. Use turpentine or mineral spirits to remove oil-base paints, enamels, and varnish; alcohol to remove shellac; and special solvents to remove lacquer. Remove latex paints promptly from brushes with soap and water. If any type of paint is allowed to dry on a brush, a paint remover or brush-cleaning solvent will be needed.

Using a Spray Gun Spray guns are particularly useful for large areas. While the conventional type of compressor/gun setup is difficult to control for interior work, the airless spray arrangement is ideal. Once you have perfected the spraying technique as directed by the manufacturer, you can produce a coating with excellent uniformity in thickness and appearance at a very fast application speed. In many localities, airless spray equipment can be rented on a daily or weekly basis from paint dealers or tool rental shops.

Other Painting Accessories To make your cleanup job easier, drop cloths should be used when painting. For smaller jobs, newspapers can serve the same purpose as drop cloths. Plastic drop cloths can be purchased in most paint and hardware stores. Because of their light weight, these plastic drop cloths tear easily, shift easily, and can bunch up. You would probably be wise to purchase this type of drop cloth if you are not planning on using it more than just a few times. If you intend to do a great deal of painting, however, you can purchase a canvas painting tarp. These are generally 9 by 12 feet and will withstand years of handling.

A

C

B

D

Cleaning a brush: (A) Loosen trapped paint with your fingers and allow the brush to soak in the proper solvent;

(B) Wash the brush in warm soapy water and rinse; (C) Twirl out excess water and (D) comb the bristles.

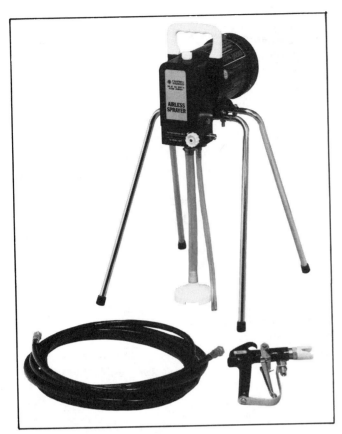

An airless paint sprayer.

A paint scraper will be needed for much of the surface preparation work you must do. The best type to use is the flat-edged variety with a 3- or 4-inch-wide blade. If the edge ever becomes dull, you can file it back to the proper sharpness.

Ladders are one of the most common painting accessories—and also the most dangerous. Many painting accidents occur because proper ladder

A plastic painting drop cloth.

safety procedures are not followed. Whether you have a wooden or aluminum ladder, always keep it in top condition. Inspect the ladder before each use. The rungs or steps should be solid and the ladder locked open. Make sure that the ladder is on a firm surface and is level. A rocking ladder can easily throw you off balance. Always keep one hand on the ladder to steady yourself. Work facing the ladder, not with your back to it; the same applies for climbing up and down. Never stand on the top of a ladder. If you lose your balance, there is nothing for you to hold on to. Never climb higher than the second step from the top. If you find you have to go higher to complete the work, you should either purchase or rent a larger ladder.

Proper stance for working on a ladder.

Surface Preparation

As with exterior painting, preparation for interior work depends on the surface and its condition. For example, the amount of wall preparation needed will depend on whether you are working with new walls or old ones that have had a previous treatment. If it is an old surface, the preparation needed will depend on whether the surface is plaster, wallboard, or wood, and on the type of finish used previously. In general, the walls should be clean and dust-free. Remove nails, picture hangers, and other obstructions. Fill holes, cracks, and gaps between molding with spackling or some other compound. Mask off any areas that will not be painted.

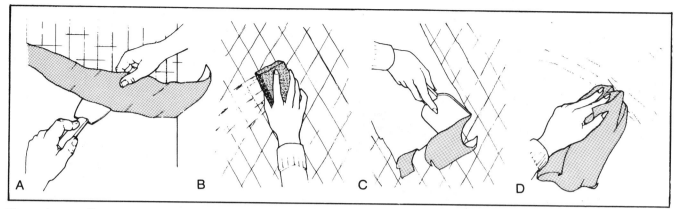

Removing wallcoverings: (A) Most vinyls can be dry stripped from the wall; for papers, (B) soak the surface, *(C) scrape off the softened paper, and (D) clean the wall.*

Previously Covered Walls You can paint papered walls if the wallcovering is well-bonded to the wall and contains no ink that will smear or stain. Test the paper by painting a small section and allowing it to dry. If paper wallcovering is torn loose from the walls in spots or has colors that will smear or bleed through the paint, take it off and clean the walls before painting. In many older homes where the paper wallcovering is layers thick, removal is essential. Other wallcovering materials must also be removed from the walls before painting. For vinyl wallcovering, start in a corner and peel it away from the wall. To remove paper, soak it thoroughly with warm water, using a large sponge or a long-handled mop to apply the water. (Steam paper-removing equipment is frequently available at tool-rental stores and is easy to use.) After the paper is softened, you can pull or tear it from the wall. If several layers of paper are on the wall, you may need to take it off layer by layer. You may need to remove stubborn areas with a blunt-edged tool, such as a spatula or broad-edged putty knife. Be careful not to damage the wall. Some rough spots may require sanding. After all the paper has been removed, wash the walls with a solution of paint cleaner and warm water to remove the paste. Rinse with warm water and allow to dry thoroughly before painting.

Paper that has been painted over once before is doubly tough to remove. Take off any loose or peeling pieces, smooth the area, and leave the rest alone. Trying to remove it would be a major operation.

Previously Painted Walls Walls that have been painted with a casein or calcimine paint cannot be painted again without first removing the old paint unless you use the same type of paint. Casein paint is a derivative of skim milk that comes in the form of a powder or paste. Calcimine paint has a hard, glossy chalklike look. In fact, calcimine is essentially powdered chalk and glue to which water has been added. If it is wetted in any way, it will run.

You can remove calcimine or a casein paint by washing the walls with a solution of paint cleaner and warm water. With a large sponge, begin with the ceiling and wash down the walls. When the calcimine is removed, rinse the walls with clear warm water and allow them to dry thoroughly before applying new paint. If the walls have been covered, then painted, they cannot be washed.

If the previous paint, other than calcimine or casein, is in good condition, check to see that it is free from dust, grease, or other foreign matter. A primer or seal coat is usually not needed when the painted surface is in good condition. If the old paint has a glossy finish, you may need to sandpaper the surface lightly so that new paint will adhere; otherwise peeling may result. You can also remove the old gloss with a special commercial liquid.

If it becomes necessary, you may have to strip off all of the old paint in certain areas. Apply paint remover with a brush, brushing in one direction only. Only do a small area at a time. Give it time to soften, usually several hours or whatever is recommended by the manufacturer. Use your paint scraper to remove the softened paint. Reapply the paint remover if needed. Remove the sludge and clean with coarse steel wool. Stripped areas should dry four or more hours before being painted. Wear gloves and goggles to prevent the remover from getting into your eyes. Another alternative is to use a propane torch. These, however, must be used with care. Keep a fire extinguisher handy. Just heat the

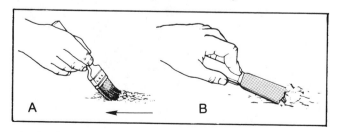

(A) Apply paint remover, brushing in one direction only. (B) When the paint softens, scrape it off.

paint to the point where it softens and then scrape. Heating cannot be used if you intend to put a clear finish on the area because it will somewhat blacken the wood.

Patching Cracks   Patch all cracks and nail holes in plaster walls before you apply paint. You can fill small hairline cracks with a spackling compound or crack filler, using a putty knife or paint scraper to put the filler in the cracks. Pick up the spackle on the paint scraper. Pull the scraper in one direction over the crack, forcing in the filler. Go back over the crack in the opposite direction to remove the excess. Let dry overnight and sand smooth. For large cracks and breaks, cut out the holes and remove the loose plaster. Cut an inverted "V" with the smallest part of the opening at the outside of the plaster surface and the largest part near the wall lath. Fill the crack with patching plaster. Dampen the edges to prevent cracking while drying. Sand the patches smooth after they are dry. For most types of paint, especially the alkyd type, plaster

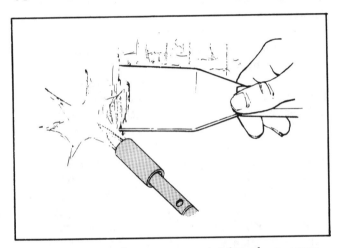

Use a propane torch to remove paint from large areas.

To repair damaged walls, remove loose material and patch the crack.

patches must have a primer or seal coat before the final coat is applied. For holes in wallboard, refer to the sections on paneling.

In the case of stains bleeding through the paint, coat the area with white shellac or white primer with a shellac base. Follow this with an oil-base or alkyd paint. For some reason, latex paints often bring the stain back through.

New Walls   The wall surface should be smooth, completely dry, and free from dust, grease spots, and any other foreign matter. Some paints cannot be applied on fresh plaster. Be sure to read the directions on your paint container to see if it can be used. Latex paint can usually be used on fresh plaster as soon as the trim is nailed. With oil-base paints, the plaster should cure for 90 days prior to painting. Or you can treat the surface with a solution of 2 pounds of zinc sulfate dissolved in a gallon of water.

Certain types of paint require the use of a primer or seal coat before you can apply them. This is especially true on plaster and wallboard because certain spots are more porous than others and will not absorb the same amount of paint. This will give a spotty final finish, or there may be areas that are glossy while others have a flat finish. A primer or seal coat will seal the pores of the wall surface and give an even absorption of paint.

Select a primer that best suits your needs for the type of paint you have chosen. If the primer you are using comes in white only, you may wish to add a little of your paint to give a better base for the final coat of paint.

Woodwork   Woodwork requires about the same preparation for painting as the walls. Whether a primer is needed will depend on the type of paint you use on new woodwork.

On previously painted woodwork, if the paint is chipped, peeling, or in bad condition, completely remove the paint. You can do this with a varnish or paint remover or by sanding. If the paint is in good condition and still has a glossy surface, sand off the gloss so that a new coat of paint can adhere to the surface.

To give a smooth surface, fill nail holes and cracks with a commercial crack filler. After the filler is dry, sand it smooth before applying the final coat of paint. Any loose pieces should be nailed down and the holes filled.

Unpainted or new woodwork to be finished with enamel or oil-base paint should be primed with an enamel undercoat to seal the wood and provide a better surface. If the unpainted wood is not primed, the enamel coat may be uneven. Unpainted wood to be finished with topcoat latex should first be undercoated. Water-thinned paint could raise the grain of the bare wood and leave a rough surface.

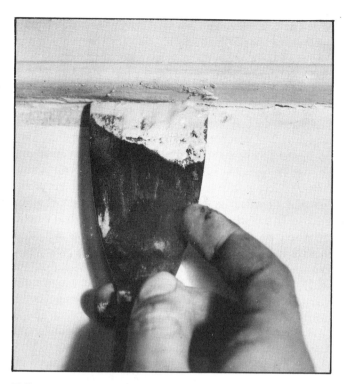

Fill in cracks around moldings.

Selection of Interior Wall Paints

Interior paints can be roughly categorized into one of three broad families: (1) flat paints that dry with no gloss and are most frequently used on walls and ceilings; (2) gloss finishes (used in kitchens, bathrooms, and on woodwork generally) that are available in various lusters from a low satin finish to a very high gloss; and (3) the primers, sealers, and undercoats that are used as bases. All of these paints are available in different grades or qualities, and many in both solvent-thinned (mineral spirits, turpentine, or benzine) or latex (water-thinned) forms.

If the woodwork is to have a clear finish, the following should be kept in mind:

1. Softwoods such as pine, poplar, and gum usually require a sealer to control the penetration of finish coats. When a stain is used, a sealer is sometimes applied first in order to obtain a lighter, more uniform color.
2. Open-grain hardwoods such as oak, walnut, and mahogany require a paste wood filler, followed by a clear wood sealer.
3. Close-grain hardwoods such as maple and birch do not require a filler. The first coat applied may be a thinned version of the finishing varnish, shellac, or lacquer.

Masonry Surfaces Smooth, unpainted masonry surfaces such as plaster, plasterboard, and various dry wall surfaces can be primed with latex paint or latex primer-sealer. The color of the first coat should be similar to that of the finish coat. But coarse, rough, or porous masonry surfaces such as cement blocks, cinder blocks, and concrete blocks cannot be filled and covered satisfactorily with regular paints. Block filler should be used as a first coat to obtain a smooth sealed surface over which almost any type of paint can be used. Unpainted brick, while porous, is not as rough as cinder block and similar surfaces and can be primed with latex primer-sealer or with an exterior-type latex paint.

An enamel undercoat should be applied over the primer where the finish coat is to be a gloss or semigloss enamel. Carefully follow the manufacturer's label instructions for painting masonry surfaces.

Latex interior paints are generally used for areas where there is little need for periodic washing and scrubbing; for example, living rooms, dining rooms, bedrooms, and closets. Interior flat latex paints are used for interior walls and ceilings since they cover well; are easy to apply by the brush, roller, or spray method; can be thinned with water; dry quickly (often within the hour); are practically odorless; and can be quickly and easily removed from applicators. Latex paints adhere to plaster, old paint, paper wallcovering, wallboard, brick, cinder block, concrete, wood, and primed metal. They can also be applied directly over gloss or semigloss enamels if the surface is first roughened with sandpaper. When using a latex, follow the label instructions carefully.

Flat alkyd paints are often preferred for wood, wallboard, and metal surfaces since they are more resistant to damage. In addition, they can be applied in thicker films to produce a more uniform appearance. Alkyds are oil-based paints that must be thinned with turpentine or solvent. They wash better than interior latexes and are nearly odorless.

Enamels, including latex enamels, are usually preferred for kitchen, bathroom, laundry room, and similar work areas because they withstand intensive cleaning and wear. They form especially hard films, ranging from a flat to a full gloss finish. Flat enamels are frequently used as undercoatings for high gloss enamels. Fast-drying polyurethane enamels and clear varnishes provide excellent hard, flexible finishes for wood floors. Other enamels and clear finishes can also be used, but unless specifically recommended for floors they may be too soft and slow-drying, or too hard and brittle. Polyurethane and epoxy enamels are also excellent for concrete floors. For a smooth finish, rough concrete should be properly primed with an alkali-resistant primer to fill the pores. When these enamels are used, adequate ventilation is essential for protection from flammable vapors.

For walls that are rough and have patched plaster, or have uneven wallboard seams, a textured finish may be used. A special paint, thicker than ordinary paint, is used for a textured finish. A heavy coat of paint is applied to the wall surface and the desired texture added while the paint is still wet. Interesting textures may be achieved by the use of a brush, sponge, or a paint roller; however, some skill is needed to obtain a regular effect.

Unless you are an experienced painter, shop for a salesperson or a paint store owner before you shop for paint. Find one who is willing and able to help you match the paint to the job. Read labels and company leaflets carefully. They are usually well written, accurate, and helpful.

Estimating Paint Quantity To determine the amount of paint needed, measure the square feet of wall area to be covered, then take these measurements to your paint dealer. The dealer should have a chart that shows the amount of paint required for the area.

To get the square feet of the wall area, measure the distance around the room. Then multiply this figure by the distance from the floor to the ceiling. For example:

Your room is 12 by 15 feet and 8 feet high.

12 + 12 + 15 + 15 = 54 feet, the distance around the room. Multiply this by the height of the wall. 54 × 8 = 432 square feet of wall area.

There are windows and sometimes doors that do not require paint, so you will deduct this space. For example, in your room there may be one door, 7 by 4 feet, and two windows, each one 5 by 3 feet. Multiply height by width to get the square feet in each.

7 × 4 × 1 = 28 square feet of door space.

5 × 3 × 2 = 30 square feet of window space.

Add these to get the total amount of space to be deducted from the room size. 28 + 30 = 58 square feet. Subtract this from the total. In other words, 432 square feet – 58 square feet = 374 square feet of wall area to be painted. Divide this number by the square footage that a gallon of the particular type of paint you have chosen will cover. The result will be the number of gallons needed for the job. Do not forget to take second coats into account. These will literally double the amount of paint needed. If the door is to be painted the same color as the wall area, do not deduct the door area.

Be sure to buy enough paint to complete the job, especially if you are having colors mixed. The second mixing may not match exactly. If the paint you choose is not available in the exact tint you want, it may be advisable to have the dealer do the mixing instead of mixing it yourself even though it may add to the cost. Careful mixing is essential to the finished product, because a paint that is not well mixed may leave an uneven, spotty appearance. When using mixed paint, try to do all of an entire wall with paint from the same can. The paint may vary somewhat from can to can. If you expect to be using all the paint within a day or so, open up all the cans and pour them into one large container such as a clean plastic bucket or garbage can. Mix the paint together and return to the original cans. Now any color variation will have been eliminated.

If you mix all the paint of the same color together, color variations will be eliminated. This is called boxing.

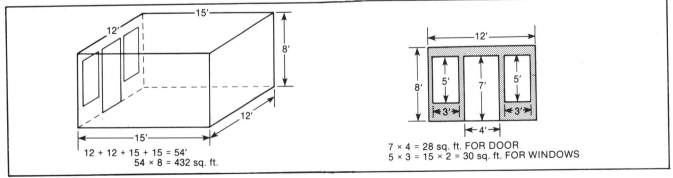

12 + 12 + 15 + 15 = 54'
54 × 8 = 432 sq. ft.

7 × 4 = 28 sq. ft. FOR DOOR
5 × 3 = 15 × 2 = 30 sq. ft. FOR WINDOWS

Find the area of the room. Subtract the square footage of doors, windows, and other areas that will not be painted.

Proper Paint Application

Before you roll, brush, or spray a drop of paint, there are certain preparations you should make to ensure a good job with a minimum of effort, errors, and spattering. The precautions may seem obvious, but they are often overlooked. For instance, read the instructions on the label of the paint container. Then move as much furniture as possible out of the room. With drop cloths, cover pieces you cannot move. Remove any hardware, such as plates over light switches, that is not to be painted over. Cover the floor with papers or drop cloths to prevent spotting. Be sure the wall and ceiling are completely free from dust and grease before you apply either the sealer or the paint.

Holes drilled in the stirrer will make it easier to mix the paint.

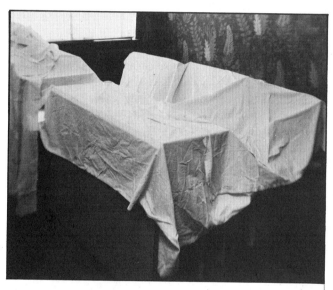

Cover any furniture remaining in the room with drop cloths before you begin to paint.

When you have assembled all the equipment and the wall is in condition for painting, read the instructions on the label of the paint container again. Follow these carefully. You can expect much better results when you do. If you are using a paint that requires a primer, apply the primer coat and allow it to dry.

Stir the paint thoroughly as directed on the label. (Be careful of the few types of paint that are not to be stirred at all.) If you will be using the paint right away, have the dealer shake it before you leave the store. This will greatly reduce the amount of mixing you will have to do. When mixing at home, drill large holes in the stirring paddle to improve its

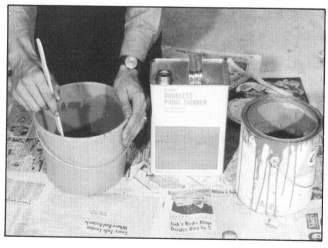

Mix thinner and paint in a separate container.

mixing ability. Do not thin paint unless absolutely necessary, then use only the thinning agent the paint manufacturer recommends. Pour some of the paint into another container to work from, unless you are using the self-feeder type of roller or spray gun. Keep the paint can tightly closed when not in use.

When you buy new paint of good quality from a reputable store, it is usually in excellent condition. However, after stirring the paint thoroughly (if it is a type that should be stirred), you should examine it for lumps, curdling, or color separation. Do not use the paint if there are still any signs of these conditions. Old paints that, upon removal of the container lid, release a foul odor (especially latex paints) or show signs of lumps or curdling, are probably spoiled and should be discarded. If there is a skin on the surface of the paint when you open the container, remove as much of the hardened film as possible with a spatula or knife and strain the paint through a cheesecloth or fine wire mesh such as window screening. An old nylon stocking also makes a good strainer. If you fail to remove the film and strain the paint, bits of the skin will adhere to your brush and the wall as you are painting. To keep paint from hardening in the rim of the can, take a tenpenny nail and punch holes all around the rim. This will allow the paint to flow back inside the can.

Punch holes around the can rim to keep paint from collecting there.

Remember to clean up paint as you go along. Wet paint is easy to remove; dry paint is hard to remove. Use turpentine or another thinner to remove oil paint and water to remove latex. Caution: If paint is dropped on an asphalt tile floor, do not attempt to remove it with mineral spirits or turpentine since this may permanently damage the tile. If the paint will not come off with a dry cloth, let it dry and then scrape it off. When you stop painting for the day, close the can and press the lid down firmly.

To keep yourself clean, rub special paint protective cream onto your hands and arms. A film of this cream will make it easier to remove paint from your skin when the job is done. Old gloves or disposable plastic gloves and aprons are also useful.

Painting Sequence

When painting rooms, do the ceilings first, walls second, then woodwork (doors, windows, and other trim). The place floors occupy in the sequence depends upon what is being done to them. If floors are simply being painted, they are done last, but if they are to be completely refinished, including sanding or scraping, do them first, then cover them with paper or drop cloths while painting the room.

The basic application techniques, brushing, rolling, or spraying, are used for most interior painting jobs.

Ceilings Prepare the ceiling as you did the walls. Generally when using a roller, work in strips the short length across the ceiling. Roll the first stroke away from you. To avoid splattering the paint, do not roll too fast, overload the roller, or spin the roller. Use a roller with a thick ¾- or 1-inch nap. This will enable you to carry more paint up to the ceiling. Slow down as you reach the wall. Ease into the junction of the wall and ceiling so as to get as little paint as possible on the wall.

If you are using a latex paint that does not show lap marks, paint a narrow strip around the entire perimeter of the ceiling. You will fill in the center area later with your roller. If you are using an alkyd paint, it is best to work across the narrow dimension of the ceiling. Start in a corner and paint a narrow strip 2 or 3 feet wide against the wall. After loading your roller, roll on a strip of the same width, working from the unpainted area into a still-wet wall-side strip. When you get to the far side of the room,

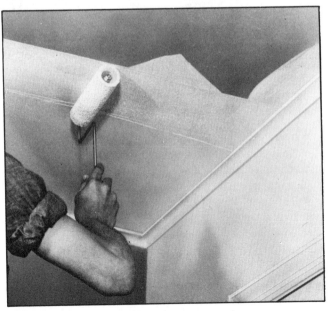

A roller makes painting the ceiling much easier. Notice that the border area between the ceiling and the wall was cut in with a brush first.

paint the area near the wall with a brush or roller and a paint guard. As you roll along, work backward into the wet edge of the previous strip. Crisscross your strokes to cover the area completely. Light strokes help to eliminate lap marks. It is a good idea to attach a tightly fitting cardboard disk around the handle of the roller to guard against any paint that may drip or run down the side of the roller.

When using a brush, also begin at a corner and paint a strip 2 to 3 feet wide across the ceiling. You may find it easier to brush on the paint and then cross-brush in the opposite direction, but always do the final brushing in the same direction. After you have completed the first strip, do another section about the same width. Continue in this manner until the ceiling is completed. Always work toward a wet edge of the last section to avoid lap marks.

You will find it easier to paint the ceiling if you place a 1½-inch plank at the proper height securely on the treads of two solidly footed, completely opened and locked stepladders. This eliminates climbing up and down several times. Make sure that for any plank over 5 feet long, you either use a double thickness of planking or reinforce the center of the plank. Of course, an even easier method is to use a long-handled roller, which permits you to paint the ceiling while standing on the floor. You may have to use a ladder only to cut in the edges.

Walls   Use the same basic procedure for painting the sidewalls as you did for the ceilings. When using a brush, start painting in a corner and complete a strip 2 to 3 feet wide from ceiling to baseboard, brushing from the unpainted into the painted area. Flat paint can be applied in wide overlapping arcs. When a few square feet have been covered, go over the area with parallel vertical strokes upward toward the ceiling. This will reduce brush marks. Work until one wall is complete. Brush marks can also be reduced if you avoid painting with a dry brush. Leave the trim and woodwork until all the walls are painted.

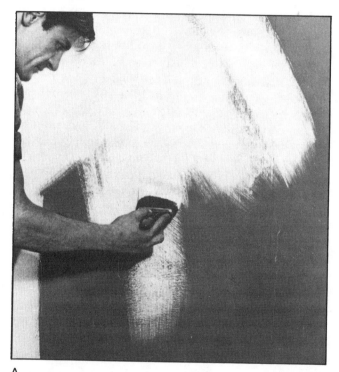

A

B

Painting a ceiling utilizing a roller with an extension handle.

Walls can easily be painted by either the (A) brush or (B) roller methods.

You cannot do a smooth paint job in the corners with a standard 7- or 9-inch roller. Therefore, unless you plan to use a special corner roller, paint the corner, top of the wall next to the ceiling, and the bottom wall next to the baseboard with a wide brush before using the roller. When using any paint other than latex, remember to do this only as you are ready to paint each strip. If the corners are allowed to dry before the inner area is painted, lap marks will show.

First paint a border with a 2-inch brush where the ceiling meets the wall. You could also use a special edge roller for this purpose. To use the roller, start about 3 feet from the ceiling and roll up, then down. Avoid rolling too fast; it causes splashes and splatters. Roll across to fill in spots you missed with the up-and-down motions. Always begin a strip by working against a wet edge. Enamels must be put on rapidly because they quickly set. Work from the top of the wall to the bottom and from corner to corner doing small areas at a time. If you need to apply a second coat, allow the paint to dry for the time recommended by the manufacturer. Check the paint in an inconspicuous spot of the last area you painted before going on to the next coat. Do not rely solely on the number of hours that have passed. Certain room conditions can speed up or slow down drying time.

All masonry surfaces should be at least eight weeks old before you even consider painting. Prepare the surface by brushing and washing. Use an interior latex paint or one of the special latexes that are made exclusively for masonry. The easiest way to paint masonry walls is with a roller. A nap of at least ¾ to 1 inch will be needed; for stucco, use the longest nap you can find. Do not roll the paint too thinly for the first coat.

Trim and Baseboards Most woodwork is painted with enamels because they do not show fingerprints and are easy to clean. If the surface has been previously stained, test the paint on a small area. If bleeding occurs, apply two coats of thinned white shellac.

When painting a double-hung window, adjust it so you can paint the lower part of the upper sash first. In this way, the inside section can be easily moved up and down. Then raise the upper sash almost to the top and finish painting the top of the upper sash. The lower sash comes next. Move the lower sash almost to the bottom. Paint top and bottom of sash and verticals. Paint the recessed part of the window frame next. After these areas have been painted, paint the mullions or the strips that hold the panes in the frame. Do the horizontal strips first and then the vertical ones. Finish by painting the sill and the frame. Do not close the window. Let the paint dry overnight. Splatters on the glass can be wiped off when wet or removed with a razor blade when dry. Other window types are painted in basically the same way.

When painting a door, remove the hardware and do the frame first. Then paint the top, back, and front edges of the door itself. If the door is paneled, paint the panels and panel molding first, starting at the top. Keep a clean cloth handy to wipe off any paint that gets on the area surrounding the panels. Paint the rest of the door last, starting at the top. Do not close the door until it is completely dry.

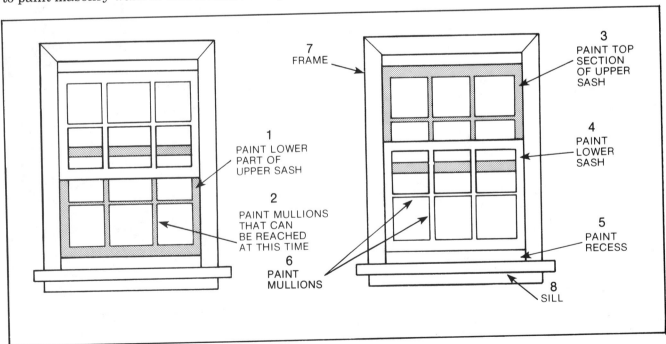

Sequence for painting casement windows.

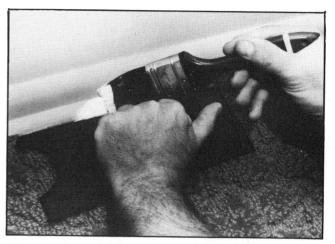

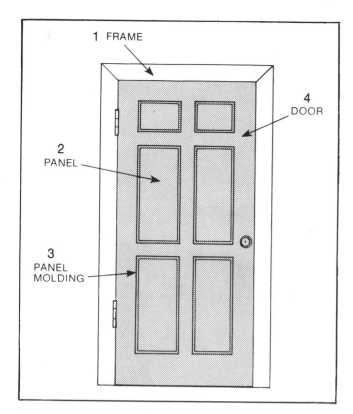

Sequence for painting a paneled door.

Use a plastic or cardboard guard when painting baseboards.

The baseboards are painted last. A cardboard or plastic guard held flush against the bottom edge of the baseboard will protect the floor and prevent dirt from being picked up in the brush. Do not let paper or a drop cloth touch the baseboard while the paint is wet.

Trim work is often painted with enamels and semigloss or gloss paints. These materials flow on more generously and with much less pressure than flat paints. Completing a small area at a time, brush on the paint with horizontal strokes, then level off with even, vertical strokes. Work quickly, but do not skip spots. Never try to go back and touch up a spot that has started to set.

Radiators should also be painted at this time. Remove any grease or rust from the outside surface and prime with red-lead paint. Only paint the visible portions of the radiator to maintain heating efficiency. Metallic paint should never be used on a radiator because it reduces heat radiation.

Textured Paint

If your walls are cracked, textured paint may be the answer to your problems. It can minimize defects that would be highly visible through other types of paint. Textured paints are available in smooth and coarse textures and can be tinted in several colors. Another coarser type of texturing

Dark molding has been added to these stucco-textured walls for a Tudor look.

that gives even better coverage can be done with joint compound.

Surface Preparation For most wall types, wash the wall with mild soap and warm water, rinse thoroughly, and let dry. Repair any defects such as gouges, hairline cracks, and dents as described in the previous chapter. With joint compound, it may be possible to ignore minor cracking because the texture will cover it. Textured paint cannot be applied over any type of wallcovering. Remove the wallcovering and then clean the walls. Prime the surface with a coat of latex paint that matches the color of the textured paint you are using. This is necessary because most textured paints do not have much masking ability.

Application of Textured Paint Textured paint can be applied with a roller or a brush. If you use a roller it will create a texture of its own. Choose one with a ¾- or 1-inch nap. Rollers work very well with the sand-textured paints. If you roll in different directions, a simulated stucco effect will be produced. Using a paint brush will give the wall a heavier texture. An interesting pattern can be achieved by patting the paint with the flat side of the brush and then pulling the brush away. Random strokes will create a rustic look. Wash your tools frequently in warm, soapy water to prevent the paint from hardening on them.

There are many other textures you can create. Generally the rougher textures are confined to ceiling applications where people will not be brushing against them. A Mediterranean look results from making short arced strokes with a notched trowel. Wet burlap, sponges, and brooms can also be used. Dampen the texturing articles before use so the paint will not stick as much to them. Some textured paints can be painted with regular latex paint after application.

For a very coarse, heavy texture, joint compound can be applied to the wall with a putty knife or a trowel. Work 12 to 16 feet at a time, and then go back and texture.

Wall Graphics

Wall graphics are full-sized designs—ranging from complex geometric shapes to simple straight and curved lines—that are painted on the wall. Not every room is suitable for a wall graphic. Modern, and in some cases contemporary, furnishings blend best with wall graphics.

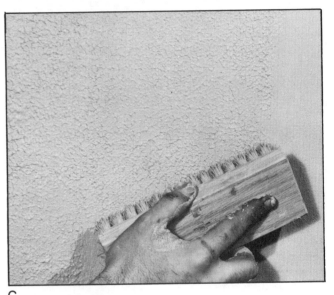

C

A

D

B

E

Texturing paint with (A) wisk broom, (B) sponge, (C) scrub brush, (D) notched trowel, and (E) corrugated cardboard.

Bold, straight and curved line wall graphic dominates the room.

Drawing the Graphic Ideas for graphics can be found in some of the many home magazines available. When it comes to actually picking a design, however, you might want to be original. First make a scale drawing of your design on graph paper. Take the dimensions and transfer the design onto the wall using a soft lead pencil. Snap chalk lines for straight areas. Circles and arcs can be accurately executed by making a string compass. Drive a small nail or tack partially into the wall where the center point of the circle or arc would be located. Tie one end of a piece of string around the nail. Tie a pencil to the other end at a point so that the length of the string is equal to the radius (half the diameter) of the completed circle. Then proceed to draw the circle, keeping the string taut. Use an artist's kneaded rubber eraser to correct mistakes.

If you have the equipment available, there is another method that makes transferring the design much easier. Draw a scale version of the design on white paper. Make sure the lines are clear and distinct. Tack the design up to a wall or use a copy stand and take a 35 mm slide of the design. Project the slide on the wall in the proper size (this may require using a different lens with the projector to get the desired enlargement) and transfer. If you color in the design on the basic drawing, you will have a good representation of how the finished graphic will look. If you use an overhead projector (the type used in schools), the same thing can be achieved by drawing the design on transparency film and projecting it.

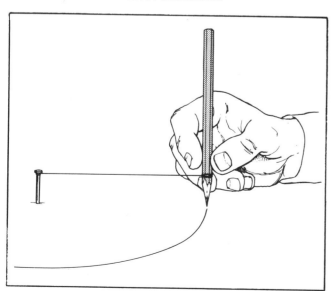

Using a string compass to make circles and arcs.

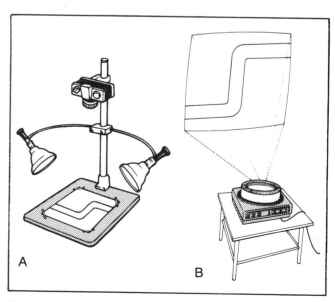

One method of transferring a graphic to the wall: (A) Take a 35mm slide of the intended graphic and (B) project it on the wall.

Painting Graphics Prepare the wall as you would for any other type of paint. If you have just painted the wall, wait at least a week before doing the graphic. In order to get crisp, clean lines when painting, use pressure-sensitive masking tape all around the outside border of the design. Where two colors meet, mask off the border and paint one color, then remove the tape, wait a week, mask the painted section, and paint the other color. (If you leave the tape in place, it will give you a line the color of the base paint separating the two. No waiting is necessary in this case.) Use 1-inch masking tape for most jobs. Thicker and thinner lines can be achieved by varying the width of the tape. Make sure that the tape is flush with the wall so no paint can seep underneath it. When removing the tape, peel it up over itself; do not pull it off. Wait until the paint is partially dry before removing the tape.

Stencils

For milder designs and borders, try stenciling. Stenciling has been a popular art in many cultures of the world. Today's stencils are easy for anyone to use and are relatively inexpensive. Precut stencils are available in a wide variety of designs and patterns. They are made from plastic so they can be used several times.

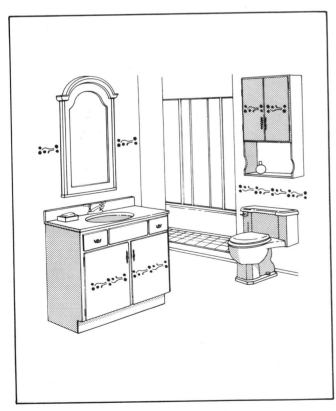

Stenciling makes a plain room exciting.

Stenciling Techniques Besides the stencil, you will also need other tools. Stencil brushes have blunt rather than tapered ends. Sizes #6 through #10 are used for most applications. The size brush you will need will vary according to the size of the openings in the stencil. Sponges and pieces of cloth can also be employed for textured applications. The best paint for stenciling is probably acrylic. Like latex paints, acrylics clean up with water. Acrylics are of a heavier consistency so there is less chance of running. Use masking tape to hold the stencil in place and to mask any areas that you do not want painted. Paper plates for mixing paint and a water container for cleanup should also be kept handy.

Latex paint provides the best surface for stenciling. Tape the stencil securely in place. Squeeze out some paint on the plate and dip the brush in it. Dab off excess on a clean area of the paint. Always work with a dry brush. Hold the brush perpendicularly over the opening and dab in the color. Work from the outside edges toward the center. A second coat may be required. When you are done applying the paint, carefully untape and remove the stencil.

Masking tape is useful for masking off areas to be painted in different colors. Mask off the first area, apply the first color of paint, and allow to dry.

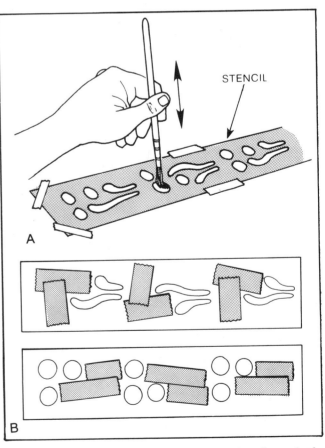

Working with a stencil: (A) Dab the paint through the holes; (B) Use masking tape to mask off areas to be painted in different colors.

Now reposition the tape over the painted area and apply the second color. To shade a design, first put on an even coat of paint. After that coat has dried, use a darker or lighter value of that color and begin to shade. Light values will highlight areas, whereas dark values will recess them. Start with the darkest or lightest color you will be using and gradually lessen the concentration until the shading blends in with the base coat. Avoid sharp breaks in value; the change should appear gradual and natural.

Common Causes of Paint Failure

Most paint failures can be attributed to some oversight during surface preparation or paint application. The surface may not have been properly prepared. For example, oil-based paint may have been applied over new plaster, or enamel surfaces may not have been roughened before the new coat was put on. It is also possible that the new paint may be incompatible with the one already on the walls. Old calcimine paints can create this problem. Dampness or leaks in the wall are another cause of paint failure. Paint, no matter how good it is, will not withstand constant exposure to moisture over any extended period.

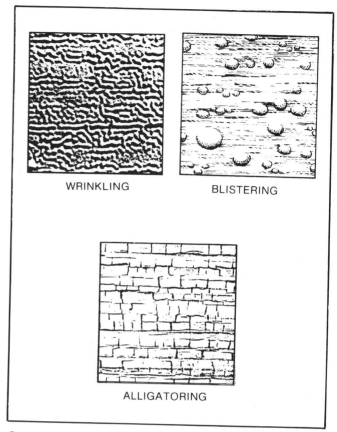

Common paint failures.

Wallcovering Selection

Wallcoverings (of which wallpaper is still number one) are one of the most versatile of all home improvement devices. They can make a room appear cozy or formal, restful or active, bright or dignified. By careful selection of colors and patterns in a wallcover, a room can be made to appear smaller or more spacious than it actually is. The ceiling can be made to appear higher or lower according to the needs of the room, and wallcover can turn a dark gloomy room into a pleasant bright one. Certain types of wallcover seem to give more character and atmosphere to a room than painted walls do.

Before selecting a wallcover, visit stores that have a wallcover department and look through every book. As you look, try to visualize the paper on your own walls. Tilt the samples in a perpendicular line so that you will see the paper as it will appear on the walls. If possible, hold two rolls side by side to get the full effect of matching the patterns.

Create with wallcoverings.

Types of Wallcoverings

Wallcoverings are available in almost any design you can think of. Floral patterns, scenics, plaids, stripes, vines, fruits, pastoral scenes, animals, birds, feather designs, geometrics, and modern abstracts are among the designs you will find. But not all wallcoverings have a pictorial pattern. Some have a textured appearance which looks like a fabric weave. Others are embossed. You will also find a selection of good solid-color papers. Special papers are made for the ceilings, and some of these harmonize in color with the sidewall patterns.

Companion papers, to be used in adjoining rooms, are also available. These coverings have different designs, but the background color is the same. Companion coverings may also be used in one room. A patterned covering may be used on one wall and a plain matching color cover on the other three walls. This is a good treatment for a long narrow room. The narrow end wall may be made to appear wider or to seemingly advance toward the center of the room.

Special features to look for in wallcovers are washability, resistance to stains, and colorfastness. Some wallcovers are more washable than others. Coverings for the kitchen or bathroom must be washable and resistant to steam vapor and grease stains. Some wallcoverings have the margins already trimmed off. This saves time and effort, but the covering will usually be a little more expensive than untrimmed paper. Other factors affecting cost are the weight and grade of the material, the number of colors, the detail of the design, and the size of the roll.

There is a wide variation in the weight and grade of different wallcoverings. Thin, low grades of paper tear easily and often stretch and wrinkle badly when wet with paste, making them hard to work with. Good grades of paper are firm and easy to handle even when wet. Extra thick, stiff paper may be a problem for the beginning paperhanger.

Before giving any advice on the selection of wallcovering for your wall, let us look at the various types available.

Traditional Wallpaper In and around 200 B.C., the Chinese were already covering their walls with paper. Wallpaper has been in existence since then. Despite its longstanding popularity and relative inexpensiveness, however, paper presents one major problem: It is generally not washable unless treated with a special plastic coating. Minor marks can be removed using an artist's kneaded rubber eraser which lifts up dirt without pulling up too many paper fibers, but this is not one hundred percent effective. Keeping this fact in mind, do not use wallpaper in kitchens, bathrooms, or playrooms where it will be subject to dirt, grease, moisture, and fingerprints. Instead, save wallpaper for the dining room, living room, or adult bedroom where the wear and tear will not be so great. Wallpaper is available in various solids and patterns that can be matched to any decor.

Save paper wallcoverings for less trafficked areas such as the dining room.

Vinyls Vinyls were the big revolution in wallcoverings. Vinyls come in a variety of patterns, colors, and textures. Best of all, vinyls wipe clean with a damp cloth. Vinyl wallcoverings have a paper or fabric backing, but the surface is actually a thin coat of plastic. Many vinyls are able to be drystripped; that is, they simply can be peeled off the wall when it comes time to redecorate. The backing that remains on the wall acts as a liner for the new wallcovering. Prepasting is another plus feature of many vinyl wallcoverings, eliminating the time wasted and the mess of spreading paste. If the vinyl is not prepasted, special vinyl adhesives will be required. Special vinyl-to-vinyl adhesives are also needed for any overlapping areas.

Wet-Look Vinyls Wet-look vinyls are similar to regular vinyls except that they have a glossy surface much like high-gloss enamel paints. There are several things you should consider before hanging these wallcoverings. Like the gloss paints they

resemble, these vinyls will reflect light and produce a glare. Do not use them near a heavily lighted (naturally or artificially) work area where the glare could impede your vision. If the walls of the room are very bumpy, you should avoid using wet-look vinyls at all. These wallcoverings tend to accentuate every bump, hole, and crack in the walls. Fingerprints and scratches will also stand out. For minor bumps, use lining paper. Wet-look vinyls can be wiped clean with a nonabrasive type cleaner.

Cushioned Vinyls These materials, installed similarly to regular vinyl wallcovering, have recently come on the market. Cushioned vinyl is sold by the roll, can be installed over nearly any material, and is fire and stain resistant. Its most frequent use is in bathroom installations.

Cushioned vinyl used as a tub surround.

Tufted Vinyls Soft tufted vinyls can add the look of rich leather or luxurious crushed velvet to your walls in diamond, button, and other geometric patterns. They are easy to clean, durable, and provide good sound absorption. They are frequently seen in offices, bars, dens, and other recreational areas.

Foils and Mylars Foils are thin sheets of metal foil attached to a paper or fabric backing, whereas mylars have a thin coating of polyester as a surface. Most of the problems found with wet-look vinyls also apply to these two wallcovering types. They both wipe clean, but will show fingerprints, wiping marks, scratches, and bumps very readily because of their smooth surfaces. This is especially true of the foils because of the reflective surface.

One advantage of using foils, however, is that they make the room look much deeper than it actu-

Tufted vinyl can be combined with paneling, paint, or another type of wallcovering.

Grasscloth and Cork   Grasscloth and cork are both delicate wallcoverings and, as such, should be kept out of busy areas. If traditional wallpaper can be called hard to clean, then these are even more troublesome since the textures trap dirt. Grasscloth, or woven grass, and cork are natural products that have been glued to paper backings. If you want to use either in a kitchen or bath setting, hang it on a wall that is not near fixtures or appliances and use complementary vinyl wallcoverings on the other walls.

Fabrics and Burlaps   Fabrics and burlaps, since they are not washable, should be reserved for areas in which you want to create a special effect such as in a bedroom. You must use a nonstaining paste when hanging these wallcoverings, and they must actually be preshrunk before they are used.

Synthetics   These are a new breed of durable wallcoverings that are able to be dry-stripped. They have the advantage that they do not shrink or stretch so there is less problem with seams opening.

Sisal   These natural wallcoverings are made of woven sisal, a fiber taken from the Mexican agave plant. Because of their rough texture, they can be used to effectively cover up rough wall areas.

ally is. Foils simulate the effect produced by using an entire wall of mirrors, but the reflection from the foils is much easier on the eyes.

Flocks   Flocks have raised nylon fibers applied to the surface of a paper or a foil to simulate the look of cut velvet. Very popular in formal settings, flocks grace rooms in palaces and state buildings. They provide a rich look that can well serve your dining area or bedroom at home as well. To clean flocked paper, simply use the soft brush of your vacuum cleaner. Brush in one direction so the nap is all laying in the same way. Just treat the flocking gently to prevent the small fibers from coming loose. Like traditional papers, flocks do not hold up well in areas of heavy use.

Designs

With wallcoverings, you not only have a multitude of colors with which to experiment, but you also have design variations. Although plain, solid-colored wallcovering may be more to your liking, wallcovering is available in a multitude of stripes,

Typical flocked wallcovering.

Woven sisal wallcovering applied to a fireplace wall.

patterns, and florals. You can use two complementary patterns together, a pattern and a solid, or one overall pattern. The choice is up to you. A few of the patterns you can expect to see when flipping through a sample book are outlined in the following paragraphs.

Damasks   If you like flocked wallcoverings, the one you choose could likely be a damask pattern. Damasks generally have one central motif that is caged in by lacy latticework. Many are done in an analogous color scheme.

Old damask pattern.

Florals   Florals are some of the most popular wallcovering designs. You can use florals almost anywhere: bright vinyl florals in the kitchen and bath, a formal floral in the dining room, a translucent watercolor floral in the living room, and a small dainty floral in the bedrooms. A smaller piece of floral wallcovering could even be hung on a plain

An example of an allover floral.

wall and bordered to look like a picture. Remember—florals are not for women only.

Geometrics   Stripes, polka dots, checks, plaids, and diagonals are all geometric designs. These can be formed with shades and tints of one color or be multicolored. You can be as bold as you wish. Op-art designs, creating visual illusions, became popular in the mid to late 1960s. These are the very bold geometrics that are often done in black and white; black, white, and the three primary colors; or fluorescent colors. The one problem with op-art geometrics is that they can become very hard on the eyes after extended viewing.

Geometric designs can create different optical effects.

Paisleys   Paisley patterns (the swirling cones, cypress trees, and leaves) have long been popular on shawls, skirts, and ties. When used for wallcoverings, the paisley design, which originated in India, gives the mysterious aura of the Far East. These rather intricate designs should be saved for formal locations. Otherwise, they tend to look out of place and lose some of their aesthetic appeal.

Elaborate paisley print.

Toiles　The true toiles combine landscapes and figures in various pastoral settings. The line engravings are generally done in one color, either brown, green, or red. These French prints usually work best in dining areas, but can be used in other locations as well. If you use one in the dining room, try painting the woodwork and dadoes in white or off-white for a French neoclassic look.

Toiles tend to depict outdoor or country scenes.

Murals　Murals can be considered a refinement of the French toiles. Unlike the toiles, however, murals can have any of a variety of subjects from a one-panel London call box to a full wall view of a Mediterranean beach at sunset. Some murals are photographlike reproductions, while others are clearly drawings. Once confined to restaurants, murals are being seen more and more in homes as devices to set a theme or tone for a room. Murals are simply panels of wallcovering that are matched to form a picture and are just as easy to install.

Textures/Sculptures　Although we can consider textures as patterns, they are really in a class by themselves. They bridge the gap between plain solids and the more distinct patterns. Textures can be real or simulated. In other words, you could purchase grasscloth or vinyl that is embossed to look like grasscloth but is much easier to clean. The textures may be those of cork, burlap, bamboo, brick, wood, or many other natural materials. Some strongly embossed, sculptured papers can even simulate the look of pebbles or old tin scrollwork. This latter type is especially good for concealing old, bumpy walls and can even be painted over without any harmful effects.

A

B

(A) Photographic mural of the Grand Canyon and (B) fragile, drawn floral branches.

Sculptured wallcoverings are available in embossed patterns that resemble old tin scrolls.

Matching a Pattern

All the designs or patterns mentioned can be broken down into three pattern types. The pattern type will give you a good clue as to how easy the wallcovering will be to hang and match. The three pattern types of which you should be aware are: straight across, drop, and random.

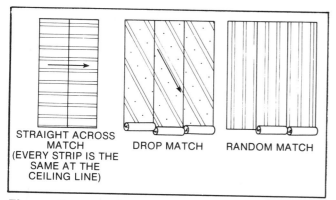

STRAIGHT ACROSS MATCH (EVERY STRIP IS THE SAME AT THE CEILING LINE)   DROP MATCH   RANDOM MATCH

Three pattern match types.

Straight Across In straight across matches, the pattern repeat goes horizontally across the strips. Plaids and horizontal stripes are good examples of straight across matches. Also note that in this type of match, every strip will be identical at the ceiling line. For this reason, start with a whole section of the pattern. Split patterns are not aesthetically pleasing. The beginning wallcover hanger will find that the straight across matches will be the easiest ones with which to work.

Drop Rather than running straight across, drop matches run either up or down diagonally. The design is staggered so that only every other strip will match at the ceiling line, such as in diamond patterns. While drop match patterns are often used in the more interesting wallcoverings, the beginning wallcover hanger may find it difficult to follow the pattern continuation.

Random There is no specific across-the-strips match in random patterned wallcoverings as is the case with vertical stripes, simulated paneling, and textures.

Effects with Designs and Patterns

As was described in the first chapter on color, a pattern can also change the visual impact of a room. Vertical stripes will make a ceiling seem higher, especially if the ceiling is done in a light color. Horizontal stripes, on the other hand, bring down the height of the ceiling. Horizontal stripes can also be

Vertical and horizontal stripes can visually alter the dimensions of a room.

used to make a narrow room seem wider because they appear to push the walls apart. But select striped patterns with care. A covering with great contrast in color or value of the stripe and the background may become tiresome. Extremely high ceilings can also be made to appear lower by stopping the side wallcovering a foot or so below the ceiling and treating the rest of the wall the same as the ceiling.

Choosing the correct design can also enable you to work with the size of the room. Large bold patterns and dark colors work well in a large room, but they can make an already small room look even smaller. Light solid colors and small designs make small rooms seem larger. Small delicate patterns may seem lost in large rooms.

Use a colored, airy design if you do not want to stick with a solid color. You can also use a textured wallcovering on two walls and a patterned one on the others. You should avoid using two strong patterns in the same room because it creates visual confusion. Also, do not use a patterned wallcovering in

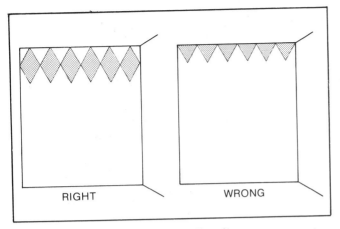

RIGHT   WRONG

Never break a pattern at the ceiling line.

a room that is heavily furnished. It will produce a cluttered effect, and the room size will appear visually reduced.

If you discover that the walls in a particular room are very uneven, do not select a wallcovering that has strong stripes like plaids, checks, or lattice patterns. These emphasize the crookedness. Instead, stick with an allover pattern that will draw the eye from the faults. Allover designs are also useful in concealing minor chips, cracks, and imperfections. Remember: Never break a pattern at the ceiling line. It creates a feeling of uneasiness.

When selecting a wallcovering, consider the activities taking place in a room. Quiet delicate designs and colors are more appropriate in rooms intended for sleeping, resting, reading, and conversation. The living room and bedrooms usually fall in this category. For more active rooms, such as the den and family room, more bold, vivid designs and colors may be used. Because the hallway and the dining room usually are not occupied for long periods of time, they may have more outstanding patterns and colors. Kitchen walls should be cheerful and restful. Avoid a spotty scattered pattern and the too-realistic designs that copy nature in every detail. A conventionalized or stylized design is more satisfactory over a long period of time.

As stated earlier, warm colors, such as tints of red, pink, yellow, orange, and yellow-green, give a feeling of warmth to a room. They have a stimulating effect and make a room appear smaller than it really is. The cool colors, green, blue, cool gray, lavender, and blue-green, are receding and make a room appear a little larger. These colors are restful and good to use on walls of rooms that get too much sunlight.

Consider woodwork as a part of the background and avoid great contrasts between the color and value of the woodwork and walls. Contrasting colors emphasize the woodwork and tend to break the room into different areas of walls, windows, and doors. Painting woodwork the same color as the background or the predominant color in the wallcovering helps to tie the woodwork and walls together and make a unified background for the room furnishings.

Well-designed wallcovering may be the source of a color scheme for a room, and it can tie together all the colors used in a room. Wallcovering for a room should be harmonious in color and design with that of other rooms or hallways that open into it. In selecting paper for the ceiling, remember that a light-colored ceiling reflects more light than a dark one. A glossy-surface paper will produce more glare than will a soft, nonglossy paper.

Estimating the Amount of Wallcovering Needed

To estimate the amount of wallcovering required for a job, keep in mind that the roll is a standard unit of measurement in the wallcovering industry. The material may come in double A or triple A roll bolts, but the roll is still the standard unit of measurement, and each roll contains approximately 36 square feet. However, when hanging the material you will always have a certain amount of waste while trimming and cutting the strips to size, so you will actually obtain approximately 30 square feet of usable material from each roll.

To figure how many rolls you will need for a given room, first measure the distance around the room. Then multiply this figure by the distance from the baseboard to the ceiling. This will give the number of square feet of wall area. For example:

Your room is 15 by 20 feet and 8 feet high.

15 + 15 + 20 + 20 = 70 feet, the distance around the room. Multiply this by the height of the wall. 70 × 8 = 560 square feet of wall area. But there are doors and windows that require no paper, and you must deduct this space. For example, in your room, there are one door, 7 by 4 feet, and two windows, each one 5 by 3 feet. Multiply height by width to get the square feet in each.

7 × 4 × 1 = 28 square feet of door space

5 × 3 × 2 = 30 square feet of window space

Add these to get the total amount of space you will deduct from the room size.

28 + 30 = 58 square feet

Subtract this from the total, 560 square feet – 58 square feet = 502 square feet of wall area to be papered.

Now, divide this figure by 30; this room would require approximately 17 rolls of wallcovering. Estimate the number of rolls of ceiling covering needed in the same way, multiplying the length of the ceiling by the width to get the square feet.

This attic was fully insulated between rafters and on outside walls, then covered with paneling. The series of platforms, which eliminates the need for furniture, is partially finished with the paneling to strengthen the built-in look. The paneling was installed both horizontally and vertically to create contrast. Photo courtesy of Champion Building Products

The sloping roof commonly found in the attic can pose several wallcovering design problems. Here several materials are combined to create an attractive bedroom and recreation area. The bedroom walls and ceiling are finished with light-colored paneling. The dark paneling on the recreation area walls provides excellent contrast to the white painted ceiling. Photo courtesy of Selz and Seaboldt

Paneling style can help set the tone of a room. The weathered wood paneling (above) enhances the used-brick fireplace and white stucco ceiling to create a rustic, Colonial appearance. The built-in cabinets were constructed of the same material. Photo courtesy of Vermont Weatherboard

Paneling can be applied in several ways. In the family recreation area (below) paneling was applied vertically below the chair molding and horizontally above it. This creates interest within large wall areas. Photo courtesy of Georgia Pacific

Knotty pine paneling was used in this remodeled family room (above) to blend with the pine boards used around windows and as trim. The entire room appears constructed of the same material. Photo courtesy of Congoleum

In the bathroom (below) the blue gray paneling was used on the walls, on cabinet-door surfaces, and on the bathtub surround and toilet enclosure. The paneling highlights the color of the fixtures. Photo courtesy of Kohler

A very popular, but somewhat expensive, bathroom wallcovering is cedar or redwood planks and boards. The wood is very durable, requires little maintenance, and tolerates moisture very well. Cedar planks were used in the bathroom shown below. The cedar and ceramic tile create a warm appearance and result in a bathroom that is easy to clean. Photo courtesy of Hedrich-Blessing

Pine boards and logs create a natural setting. Natural woods generally require little maintenance. The wood used in the kitchen (above right) helps create a light, airy appearance and blends nicely with the cabinets. The handsome den (lower right) features pine-log walls and a pine-plank ceiling. Photos courtesy of Pan Abode Cedar Homes

Wood planks and boards can be installed three ways: horizontally, diagonally, or vertically. In the above bathroom tongue-and-groove pine boards were used horizontally for enclosing the shower/sauna area and for the back wall. Photo courtesy of Pan Abode Cedar Homes

A fireplace was added to the corner of this master bedroom/bathroom (right). The walls were painted white to match the ceramic tile surrounding the bathtub and to balance the dark color of the exposed log wall and floor. Wallcovering was used at the top of the wall to add color and interest. Photo courtesy of Eljer Plumbingware

Wood planks and boards are available in a variety of colors and shades. Plan to finish walls with boards that will complement existing design elements, such as cabinets, appliances, and fixtures. The cabinets and wood walls are the same tone in the kitchen at left. Photo courtesy of Pan Abode Cedar Homes

A strong color was needed to provide interest in the predominantly white bedroom at left. A dark green was selected for the far wall and the walls surrounding the recessed toilet and towel storage area. Photo courtesy of Eljer Plumbingware

The white kitchen (above right) needed a strong bright color to serve as an accent. An orange color that closely matches the sink fixture was selected. Photo courtesy of McKone and Co.

The monochromatic color scheme of this kitchen (lower right) was designed with one purpose in mind: to create a pleasant, cheerful room. Photo courtesy of Armstrong Cork Company

The monochromatic color scheme in the family room (below) creates a bright, attractive room that takes advantage of the southern exposure by means of the floor-to-ceiling windows. Photo courtesy of Congoleum

The kitchen (above) was painted a light cream color to enhance the beautiful woodwork, brick trim, and ceramic tile
floor. The result is a natural, Colonial-style kitchen. The
light, plain color of the paint allows the darker wood trim,
doors, and furnishings to stand out.

Simple molding on a painted surface can create a beautiful
area (above right). The molding can be painted a contrasting
color or the same color as the background. Photo courtesy of
Western Wood Moulding

Coordinated wallcoverings can be used together to create an
attractive room design (lower right). Photo courtesy of SK
Advertising

The dark blue wallcovering and exposed timbers in the bathroom at right create a masculine appearance. Photo courtesy of Eljer Plumbingware

The pattern for this subtle, earthtone wallcovering (far left) is matched horizontally. To achieve this, whole sections of the floral pattern were started in the same relative position along the ceiling line. Photo courtesy of Sherwin Williams

Creating the complex design around the window (near left) requires care and time, but the result can be very attractive. Photo courtesy of American Olean

Bold geometric patterns generally look best in large rooms or open areas. A washable wallcovering was used between cabinets in this kitchen (lower left). Note the matching curtains. Photo courtesy of Boise Cascade

Two wallcover patterns were combined in this beautiful monochromatic design (below). Vinyl was used because of its easy maintenance. Photo courtesy of Armstrong Cork Company

Wallcovering patterns can be as dominant or subtle as desired. The abstract circular pattern in the above kitchen is dominant but contrasts well with the red cabinets. Photo courtesy of Yorktowne

The textured pattern in the kitchen (above right) is subtle but enhances the cabinet grain and the ceramic tile pattern. Photo courtesy of Wilsonart

The pattern in the bedroom (below) is subtle, but the color blends well with the other design elements in the room. Photo courtesy of Hedrich-Blessing

The strong floral pattern in the bathroom (lower right) commands attention and effectively complements the colors of the bathtub and its enclosure. Photo courtesy of Kohler

Several new materials have been adapted for wall use in recent years. Of these, ceramic tile (above) is one of the most popular for bathrooms and kitchens. Photo courtesy of American Olean

Mirrors are gaining in popularity as wall surfaces. This small bathroom (below) was made to look much larger by covering two walls with mirrors. Photo courtesy of Hedrich-Blessing

Stone and imitation stone are popular wallcovering materials. Slate was used around the fireplace in the living room above. Photo courtesy of Hedrich-Blessing

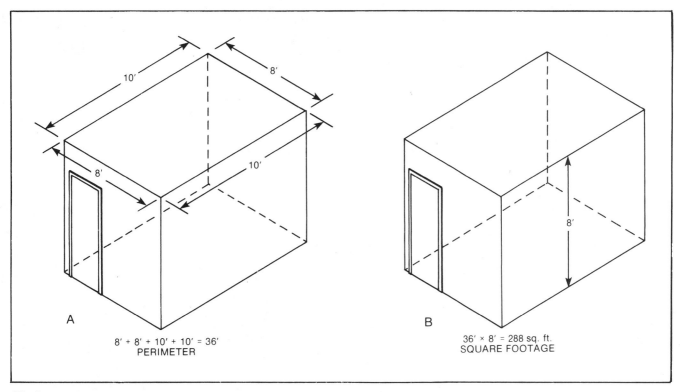

8' + 8' + 10' + 10' = 36'
PERIMETER

36' × 8' = 288 sq. ft.
SQUARE FOOTAGE

Finding the perimeter and then the square footage of a room.

For a quick reference aid in estimating the amount of coverage needed for a single wall and four walls, see the tables given on pages 50 and 52.

When purchasing your wallcoverings, be sure all the bolts have the same style number and run number marked on them. The run number is similar to the dye lot number on yarn and will assure a close color match. Record these numbers in an easily located place in case you need to purchase more of the same wallcovering.

In addition to wallcovering material, you will need the following materials and equipment for doing a good job of paperhanging: a ladder to reach the ceiling; a large flat surface or table; a large pail for paste; a brush or paint roller for applying paste; a smoothing brush to smooth the paper on the wall (a fiber brush about 10 inches wide or a clean clothes-brush will do); a rotary beater or similar device to mix the paste; a pair of large sharp shears; a trimming knife or razor blade to trim the wallpaper; newspapers to cover the table while applying paste; wallpaper paste, unless you are using prepasted wallpaper; a yardstick or T-square for measuring straight edges; and a plumb line (long string with weight tied to one end). If the walls need repairing, you may need patching plaster to fill the holes and cracks, a putty knife, paperhanger's size, a scraper, and sandpaper.

Kits containing tools needed for hanging wall-coverings are available at wallcovering stores, often on a rental basis.

Preparing the Wall

No wallcovering job will be better than the surface on which the covering is hung. The walls must be properly prepared for the wallcovering to hang smoothly and look good for a long period of time. The preparation needed depends on the type of finish the walls have had previously, the material of the wall, and whether the wall is new or old.

Before doing any work on the walls, turn off the electricity and remove switch and wall outlet plates as well as light fixtures.

Papered Walls and Ceilings   If the old paper is in good condition, well bonded to the wall, and in not too many layers, you do not need to remove it. You can put new paper over the old without resizing the wall.

If the paper is loose in just a few places, remove it and sand the edges of the hole smooth with sandpaper. When bare plaster is exposed, size it and allow the sizing to dry before applying a new covering.

Completely remove old paper that is in poor condition. You can do this as described in an earlier chapter. After all the paper is off, wash the walls with a solution of paint cleaner and warm water to remove all the paste. Rinse with warm water and allow the walls to dry thoroughly.

Fill cracks or holes with patching plaster, then apply a coat of size to the entire wall. You can buy wallcovering size at a paint store, complete with

Room and Ceiling Estimating Chart						
Distance Around Room in Feet	Corresponding Room Area Measurement in Feet	Single Rolls* for Wall Areas According to Ceiling Height			Number of Yards for Borders	Single Rolls for Ceilings
		8′	9′	10′		
28	6 x 8	8	8	10	11	2
30		8	8	10	11	2
32	6 x 10, 8 x 8	8	10	10	12	2
34		10	10	12	13	4
36	6 x 12, 8 x 10	10	10	12	13	4
38		10	12	12	14	4
40	8 x 12, 10 x 10	10	12	12	15	4
42		12	12	14	15	4
44	8 x 14, 10 x 12	12	12	14	16	4
46		12	14	14	17	6
48	10 x 14, 12 x 12	14	14	16	17	6
50		14	14	16	18	6
52	12 x 14	14	14	16	19	6
54		14	16	18	19	6
56	12 x 16, 14 x 14	14	16	18	20	8
58		16	16	18	21	8
60	12 x 18, 14 x 16	16	18	20	21	8
62		16	18	20	22	8
64	12 x 20, 14 x 18	16	18	20	23	8
66		18	20	20	23	10
68	14 x 20, 16 x 18	18	20	22	24	10
70		18	20	22	25	10
72	14 x 22, 16 x 20, 18 x 18	18	20	22	25	12
74		20	22	22	26	12
76	16 x 22, 18 x 20	20	22	24	27	12
78		20	22	24	27	14
80	16 x 24, 18 x 22, 20 x 20	20	22	26	28	14
82		22	24	26	29	14
84	18 x 24, 20 x 22	22	24	26	30	16
86		22	24	26	30	16
88	20 x 24	24	26	28	31	16
90		24	26	28	32	18

*Based on 30 square feet per roll.
Note: Remember to deduct one roll of wallcovering for each door or two standard-sized windows.

instructions for use. But, be sure to check the wall-covering manufacturer's directions as to the type of sizing to use. The easy way to apply size is by using a paint roller.

Painted Walls Walls that have been painted with a gloss or semigloss enamel are too slick to provide a grip for the wallcovering paste or adhesive. You can remove this gloss by sanding the wall lightly with medium-grade sandpaper or by using a commercial gloss-removing liquid. Then wash the surface using a strong washing compound, rinse it with clean water, and allow it to dry before applying a coat of size.

Walls painted with flat paints should be washed down completely with a good washing compound (for example, trisodium phosphate). This removes grease, grime, and dirt. Wash from the bottom up, and do the ceiling last.

New Plaster Walls New plaster walls should be allowed to cure for at least three months before any wallcovering is hung. On plaster walls you must watch out for hot spots, also known as alkaline lime deposits. Plaster contains lime. For security, brush the wall with an indicating wall size. The pink areas that appear are the hot spots, and these should be neutralized with a solution of one pound of zinc sulfate (available from drug stores) to a gallon of water. Let the plaster dry thoroughly and then coat with a primer-sealer.

Composition Walls or Dry Wall Construction Be sure all seams have been taped and spackled so that joinings will not show through the wallcover-

A wide variety of tools and materials come into play when installing wallcovering: (A) paste, (B) bleach, (C) buckets, (D) level, (E) cutting board, (F) drop cloth, (G) paste brush, (H) paste roller or pad, (I) spackling paste, (J) pencil, (K) putty knife, (L) razor knife, (M) sandpaper and sand block, (N) scissors, (O) screwdriver, (P) seam roller, (Q) primer-sealer and size, (R) smoothing brushes, (S) sponges, (T) stepladder, (U) plumb bob, (V) table, (W) vinyl-to-vinyl adhesive, (X) water box, (Y) wall scraper, and (Z) yardstick.

Wallcovering Estimating Chart				
Single Wall				
Length of Wall	Single Rolls for Wall Area According to Ceiling Height			Number of Yards for Borders
	8'	9'	10'	
6	2	2	2	3
8	2 to 3	3	3	3
10	3 to 4	4	4	4
12	4	4	4	5
14	4	4	5	5
16	4 to 5	5	6	6
18	5	6	6	7
20	6	6	7	7
22	6 to 7	7	8	8
24	7	7	8	9
26	7 to 8	8	9	9

Note: If the pattern you choose requires a great deal of matching, purchase the higher number of rolls.

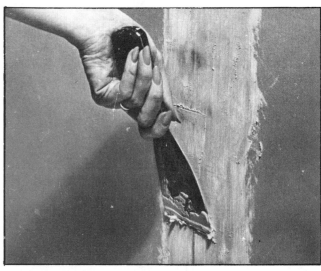

Fill dry wall joints with spackling paste.

ing. Set nails with a hammer, leaving a dent in the dry wall surface. Cover the dent with spackle and level it to the surface. Allow the spackle to dry, apply a second coat, and when it is dry, cover the unpainted dry walls with a flat primer-sealer before hanging the wallcovering. This prevents damage to the wall when the wallcovering is removed.

Scraping off old wallcovering.

Hanging Wallcoverings

The hanging of wallcovering can be divided into three basic steps: (1) preparing the paste and measuring; (2) cutting and matching the wallcovering; and (3) pasting and hanging.

Preparing Paste and Measuring

Mix the wallcovering paste or adhesive according to the instructions on the package. Mix in a large pail, but do not mix too much paste at one time. The paste should be mixed until it is free of lumps and adheres to the hand like a smooth glove. You can tie a string across the top of the paste bucket to hold the brush out of the paste when you are not using it.

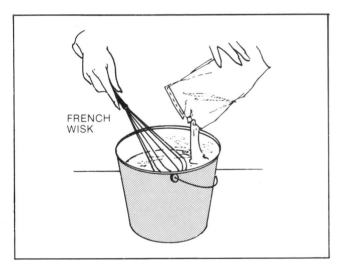

Mix the paste until it is free from lumps.

To cover the four walls of a room, the hanging operation should be started at a window or door. If you are hanging a large pattern in a room with a fireplace, center the first strip over the fireplace and work away from the fireplace in both directions. Whether the starting point is a window or door casing or a fireplace, measure along the wall to a distance that is 1 inch less than the width of the wallcovering. If, for example, the width of the paper is 24 inches, measure in 23 inches from the corner or door casing. The extra inch is to provide an overlap of the corner or casing to compensate for one that is not perfectly straight, which is usually the case.

Drop a plumb line from the ceiling to the baseboard along the mark and snap a chalk line down along the wall. To make a plumb line, hang a weight (large washer, or even your scissors) at the end of a string. Tack the string at the top of the wall so that it is closer to the starting door or window than the width of your wallcovering roll. The weight should hang just above the floor. Rub colored chalk into the string, hold the string near the weight, and snap the taut string against the wall. This will make a perfectly vertical colored chalk mark on the wall. Another plumb line should be made as each new wall is begun.

Cutting and Matching

Make all strips of the wallcovering a little longer than the ceiling to baseboard measurement to allow for matching and trimming at the ceiling and baseboard. If the covering does not require matching, cut the first strip about 6 inches longer than the measurement, then cut all the other strips the same length. Be sure a complete design is at the top of each strip. Check to see that the join marks match on each strip.

If the design must be matched, cut the first strip 8 to 12 inches longer than the ceiling to baseboard measurement, depending on the size of the design. To allow for trimming, be sure the point of the design that you want to meet the ceiling is 3 or 4 inches below the top of the strip. This assures an even line all around the ceiling. Unroll a second strip on top of and the same length as the first one, then place it alongside the first strip to see that the design and join marks match. Cut the second strip even with the top of the first strip. Cut all the strips the same way, placing each one on top of the pile with the pattern side up.

When working with patterned wallcoverings, trying to match the pattern may result in a lot of waste or scrap material. To reduce this waste, cut strips from alternate rolls of paper. For instance, take the first strip from the first roll, the second strip from the second roll, the third strip from the first roll, and continue alternating. This method reduces the likelihood that you will run short of wallcovering as you near the end of the job.

With plain or textured covering, you do not have the matching problems described for the patterned coverings. With solid colors, however, it may hap-

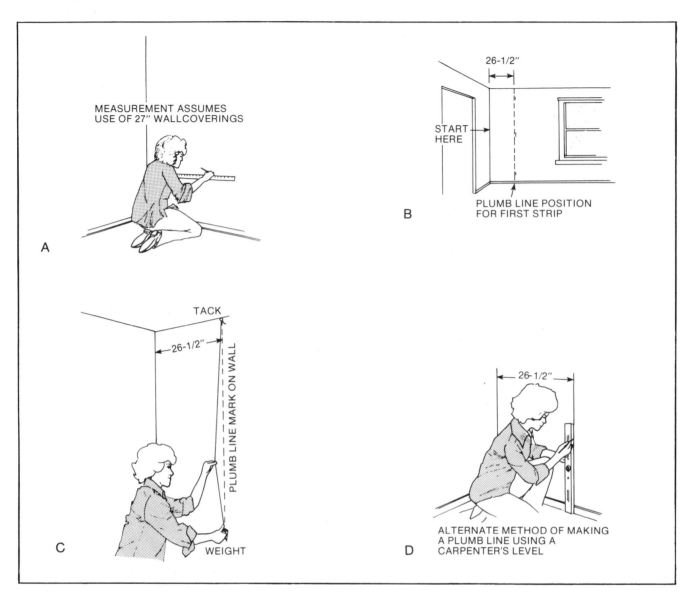

MEASUREMENT ASSUMES
USE OF 27" WALLCOVERINGS

A

26-1/2"

START
HERE

PLUMB LINE POSITION
FOR FIRST STRIP

B

TACK

26-1/2"

PLUMB LINE MARK ON WALL

WEIGHT

C

26-1/2"

ALTERNATE METHOD OF MAKING
A PLUMB LINE USING A
CARPENTER'S LEVEL

D

Procedure for making a plumb line.

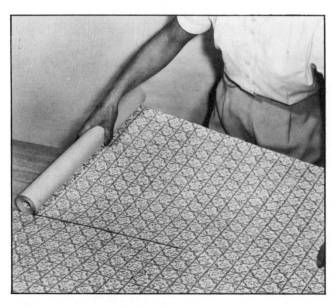

Roll out a second strip to check for pattern match.

pen that one of the roll ends will be consistently darker. To avoid a visible color lightening or deepening as your eyes progress down the wall, reverse every other strip. Putting a dark section against a light one tends to even out the appearance of the color.

When all the strips are cut, turn the pile over with the pattern side down. Trim if necessary; that is, some wallcovering has a selvage on both sides. Sometimes the dealer will trim this off for you. If he does not give this service, you can easily do the trimming. Usually one side is all that needs trimming because the next strip will lap over to cover the selvage on the other side. You may trim the selvage before applying paste to the strip or after you have folded the pasted strips together. You can trim two thicknesses of pasted paper at one time if you have the edges of the strips exactly together.

If your paper does not have a firm line to follow for

trimming the selvage, draw a line with a pencil and yardstick. You can cut the selvage with sharp shears or a trimming knife and a straightedge, such as a carpenter's square or yardstick.

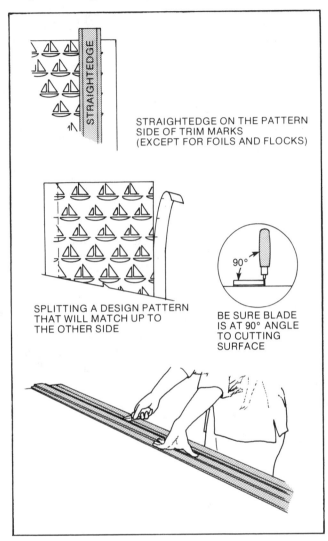

Trimming the selvage edges prior to pasting.

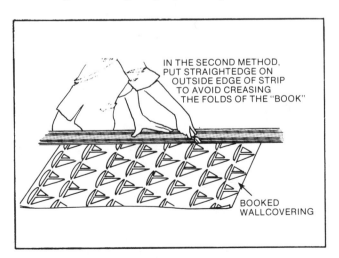

Selvage edges can be trimmed after the strip is pasted and folded, or booked, but the chance of error is greater.

Pasting and Hanging

Place the first strip, pattern side down, on a large smooth table. Apply paste to the wallcovering beginning at the top and brushing toward the bottom. When you have covered about half to two-thirds of the strip with paste, fold the top down to the center with the pasted sides together. Be sure the outside edges are exactly even. Do not crease the paper where it is folded. Next apply paste to the rest of the strip and fold the bottom up as you did the top, with the pasted sides together. This makes it easier to handle the pasted strip without danger of smearing paste on other strips. The outside edges of the strips must be even. Use enough paste. Blisters may appear later if you miss a spot.

Repeat the pasting process with each strip as you get ready to use it. Do not apply paste until you are ready to hang the strip.

Place the smoothing brush on top of the ladder so it will be handy when you need it. Now unfold the top fold of your covering. Place the strip in position where the design meets the ceiling line at the desired point, with the covering overlapping onto the ceiling. Press the covering firmly to the wall. Let the bottom fold out, and as it drops down, press it to the wall, making sure it is even with the plumb line. Place your hand flat on the paper and press it with the palm, not the fingertips. Smooth down the center first, then the edges.

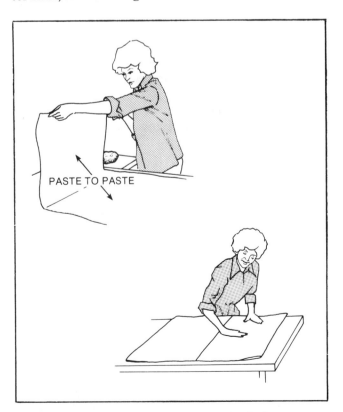

To make long strips easier to handle, book them.

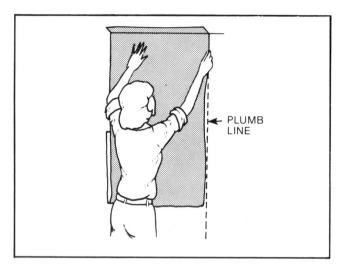

Unfold the top section of the booked strip and place it even with the plumb line.

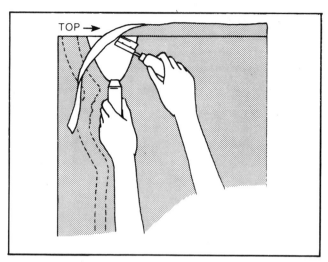

Trim off excess wallcovering with a razor knife. Use a wall scraper as a cutting guide.

When you are sure the first strip is straight, take the smoothing brush and go over the whole strip with long sweeping strokes both vertically and horizontally. If wrinkles appear, lift the bottom to where they are and brush them out. It is important that the first strip be straight.

If the left edge overlaps the frame, trim the paper with a trimming knife or make a scored line with the sharp point of the shears, then trim along the line. Trim the excess covering at the ceiling and baseboard in the same way. Push the covering firmly down around the door or window frame and baseboard.

Hang each succeeding strip in the same way, working the covering into place so that the pattern matches. Let each strip overlap the previous one about ¹⁄₁₆ inch. Roll the seams flat, using a seam roller.

After hanging each strip, see if you have smeared paste on it. If the wallcovering is waterproof, use a dry cloth. Do not allow paste to dry on the patterned side.

Hang the wallcovering over electric outlets, then take a knife or shears and cut out the area around the switches. Replace the plates. You may wish to mark the spots as you cover over them so they will be easy to find when you are ready to trim out the area.

For a decorator look, you can cover the switch plate with the wallcovering as well. Take a dry scrap of wallcovering and cut out a section that matches the pattern around the outlet. With the plate mounted, place the scrap over it, adjust it until the pattern matches, and mark the four corners with

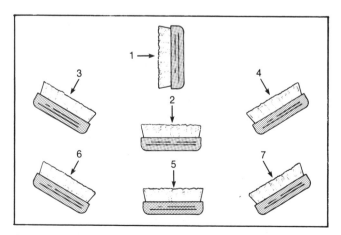

Follow the proper brushing sequence. The only horizontal stroke should be at the ceiling line.

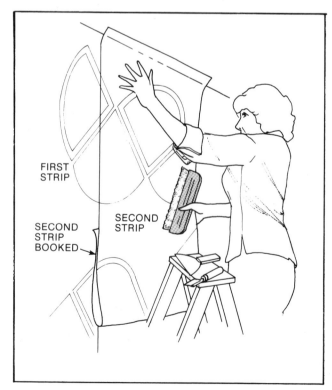

Open the top part of the strip, move it into place, and match the pattern.

Firmly roll seams if recommended by the manufacturer.

pencil dots. You might also crease the perimeter of the plate covering using the blunt edge of the scissors or your fingernail. Remove the scrap, trim so you have a 2-inch excess, and cover it and the plate with paste (or vinyl-to-vinyl adhesive if you are using vinyl wallcovering). Some plastic and chrome plates may require a prime coat so that the adhesive will hold.

If you started by hanging your covering at a door or window, there will be other doors and windows in the room that will present a different problem. To solve this problem, simply match the strip of covering to the last strip you have hung. Let the wallcovering overlap the door or window frame. Press it in place along the ceiling line and down the side that is not overlapping the frame. For a square cor-

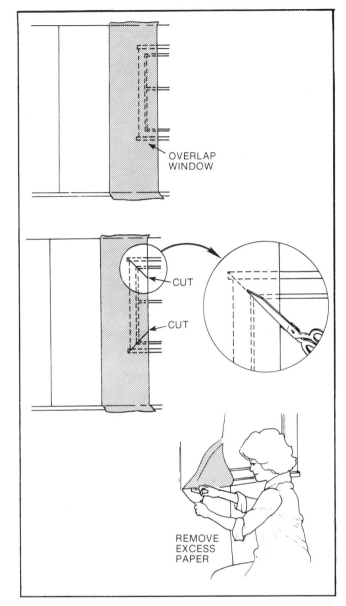

Overlap the window frame. Do not stop when you reach the edge of the frame.

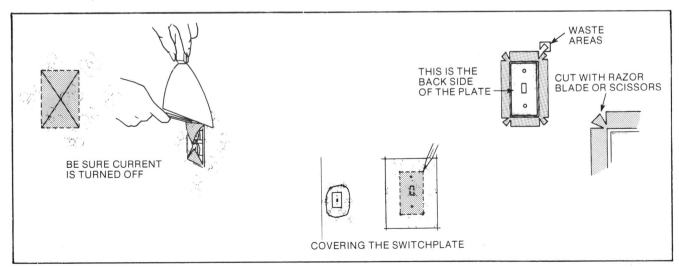

Steps in opening up and covering a switch plate.

ner, make a diagonal cut from the overlapping edge to the top corner of the frame. Crease the covering against the edge of the frame at the top and along the side. You can do this easily with the blunt edge of your shears. Then lift the paper lightly and cut off the excess paper. Press the edges firmly around the frame. Treat the bottom of the window in the same way as the top. Use a separate strip to match the center panels at the top and bottom of the windows and over the doors.

Wallcovering in the corners often buckles or splits. To prevent this, make a seam at every corner, cutting the paper to make it overlap the next wall about 1 inch. Smooth the strip in place and press it firmly into the corner, extending it about 1 inch on the adjoining wall. The next strip will overlap this extra inch.

One of the major problems when doing walls occurs in a dormer bedroom or a refurbished attic. Here, at least one wall will slant, probably two, and they can be broken up into any number of odd shapes by the roof and the windows. But such walls are less difficult to cover than they seem. The same principle of extending the material beyond the edges and at all corners applies. The necessity for cutting sections that will match as we encountered around doors and windows set flush with the walls also applies. What distinguishes the dormer situation is that, since some of the walls slant, not all the areas to be covered are rectangular. The choice of pattern becomes extremely important. Stripes will work out well, if you want a stimulating zigzag effect, but an informal scattering of flowers or branches might be better; many mismatches are inevitable where ver-

(A) Wallcovering can be wrapped, or continued, right around outside corners. Just make snips in excesses to keep the strip from tearing. (B) Ending at an outside corner.

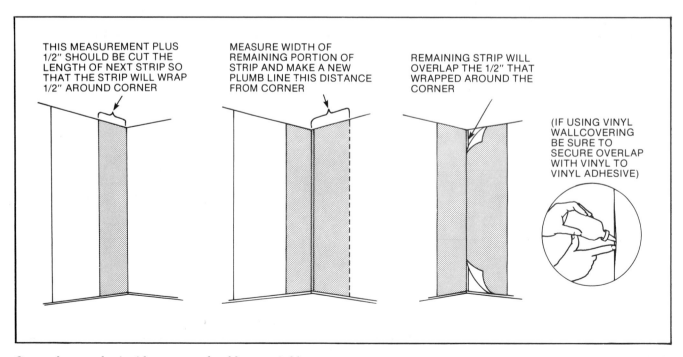

Covered properly, inside corners should not wrinkle.

tical and slanting walls meet. It is a good plan to first cut on the bias those strips that do not require trimming either at the top or bottom, just as if you were going to hang them on an ordinary straight wall. The fact that they may be placed on a slanting ceiling has nothing to do with preparing the strips. Vertical guidelines here and there will be useful, and, depending on whether or not you have a helper, you could hang these "straight" coverings beginning at the top or working up from the bottom. Or, if the room is a high one, you could hang the strips in sections. As for all the triangles that may occur in a dormer room, measure, cut, and number the strips for each position before you apply paste.

Wrapping around an archway is very similar to wrapping around an outside corner. Measure the distance from the edge of the last strip to the corner and add 2 inches. Cut your next strip to this size. The 2-inch excess will be the wrap. Hang as you would an outside corner, making sure that all air pockets are brushed out. For the wrap, cut horizontal slits at the top of the arch. Once you have the corner smoothed down, trim the wrap down to ½ inch using your razor knife and scraper. If the arch is curved rather than squared off like a doorway, make small triangular cuts about ½ inch apart on the wrap. This will eliminate any wrinkles in the wallcovering on the inside of the arch due to its curvature.

To hang the inside of an arch, cut a matching strip of wallcovering that is ½ inch narrower than the inside width of the arch. The strip should be long enough to reach from the center of the arch all the way down one side. Each strip should match the adjacent wall. Any mismatch at the top will not be noticed. Overlap the strip ¼ inch on top of the wrap.

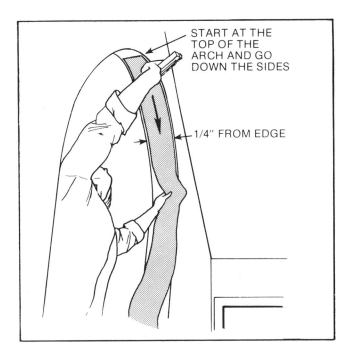

Hanging the inside of an arch.

If you have only covered the room on one side of the arch, this will leave ¼ inch of bare wall before the edge. It is important that you leave this space because it will prevent the wallcovering from fraying or peeling back at the overlapped edge. Remember that if you are using vinyl wallcovering, you should use vinyl-to-vinyl adhesive at the overlap on the inside of the arch.

In a room completely hung with wallcovering, the ceiling will be covered first, the walls next, and borders—wide or narrow—last. The merit of borders, in addition to the finishing touch they give a room, lies in their ability to conceal (or distract

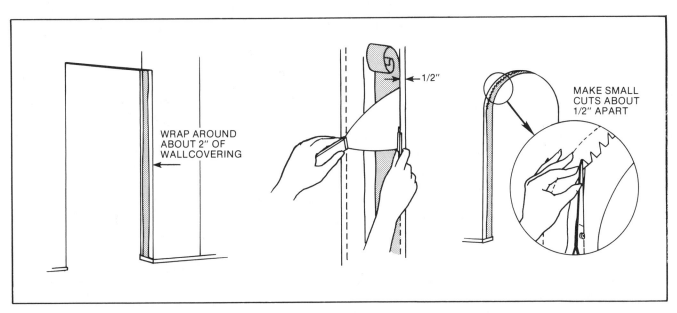

Wrapping an arch.

from) poor joining and trimming. If you know you are going to use a border at the ceiling line, you do not have to add that extra inch or two and then trim it off quite so meticulously. Borders are not as easy to find as they should be, but sometimes you can cut your own border trims from the pattern you are using, or take a narrow border from a deeper one. Wide or narrow, borders are measured and pasted like any other wallcoverings and are usually started in the most obscure corner, working from there continuously around the room. As the repeats on narrow widths are small, a mismatch at the corner where they began will not be noticeable. Small border papers used as trimming throughout a "tailored" room would be mitered like a picture frame at the corners of the doors and windows they outline.

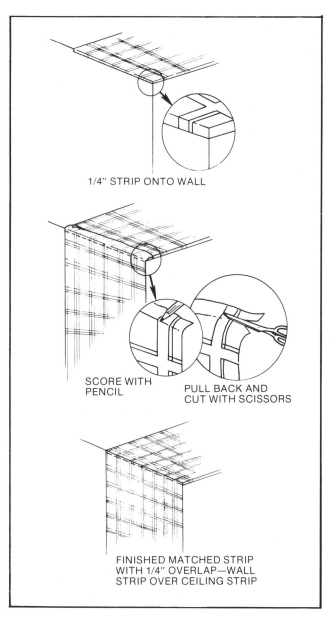

Matching a wall to the ceiling pattern.

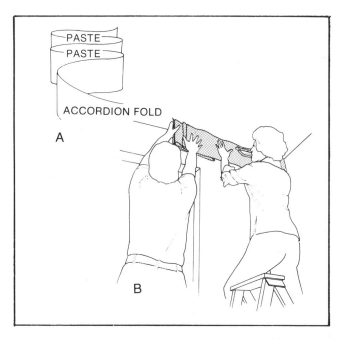

(A) Fold the border in an accordion fashion and (B) unfold the strip as the work progresses.

Covering a Ceiling As was just stated, a ceiling should be hung before the walls are. The strips should always be hung across the room, rather than lengthwise, as shorter strips are easier to handle. These strips will be cut and pasted as were those you prepared for the wall, with the same allowance of about 1½ inches at each end, that amount to be used at the top to fill in the corner where ceiling and wall join. Here the surplus covering will cut off according to what is planned: either a pattern continuing all or part way down the wall or the use of some sort of molding. If the same pattern is used on both walls and ceiling, it is an advantage when the main entrance to the room is opposite its narrow side, not its length. Then the wall pattern can be hung so that it seems to continue up and across the ceiling, adding apparent height to the room and counteracting its

shallowness. Should a guideline for the first ceiling strip be advisable, you should determine it by measuring along the short wall to a distance just less than the width of a strip of the wallcovering (so that it can overlap the edge where it starts) and employing a T-square to begin drawing the line at right angles, continuing it with a yardstick. You should plan to end the ceiling job on the less critical side of the room, perhaps just above the main entrance. The last strip will almost certainly be a partial strip, and there will be no possibility of controlling a match, if you are using a pattern.

Ceiling paper is much easier to hang when two people work together, for one person can place and smooth, while the other holds up the rest of the strip. If necessary, though, you can support the strip with a second ladder or make yourself a little scaffolding with a plank stretched between two ladders. Be sure to follow the same procedures of smoothing out wrinkles, sponging off excess paste, and trimming while the paper is wet, as you did when hanging the wallcovering.

Getting Behind Radiators After you have worked so hard to make sure that all the wallcovering edges are securely fastened, do not allow those behind radiators to hang loose. They will eventually begin to curl up from the heat and could loosen the rest of the strip. If you cannot get behind the radiator with your hand, smooth the wallcovering down with a yardstick or straightedge wrapped in cloth so it will not scratch the wallcovering. Try to trim this strip to the proper baseboard length prior to hanging.

Prepasted Wallcoverings When using prepasted wallcoverings, read the manufacturer's instructions before starting. Prepasted strips are cut and matched as are all other types of wallcoverings. Reroll the strip from the bottom to the top with the pattern inside. Roll it loosely so the water can easily reach the entire prepasted surface. Most companies furnish plastic-coated cardboard trays that you can place on the floor next to the wall. They are just the right width for the strips of wallpaper.

Check the manufacturer's instructions as to the length of time that the rolled strip should remain in the water tray. Be sure to leave each strip in the water for the same length of time so that each strip will dry and fit uniformly. Use tepid water in the water tray. Check the manufacturer's instructions as to the length of time that wallcoverings should "relax" after wetting. Place the water tray at the end of the cutting table or at the baseboard. Hang prepasted strips in the same way you would hang other wallcoverings.

Handling Special Wallcoverings

As described in the previous chapter, there are several other types of wallcoverings that can be used to beautify your home. Some of these require special application techniques.

Vinyl Wallcoverings Vinyl wallcoverings are hung much like the ordinary paper-type wallcovering just described except that special adhesives are employed and the ability to be stripped must be considered. The latter may involve the use of a lining paper for both a neater job and quicker removal. Properly hung, vinyls can be stripped off in one sheet if a corner is loosened.

When working with vinyls, you will have to be a little more careful smoothing out air bubbles and blisters behind the material since the fabric is stiffer and more airtight than ordinary paper. Many professionals use a window squeegee or broad putty

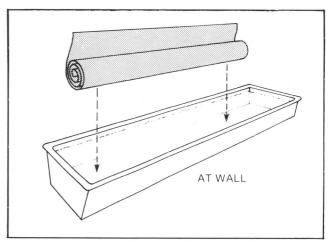

Immerse prepasted wallcovering in the water tray for the recommended length of time.

knife to smooth the vinyl against the wall, rather than the smoothing brush or sponge normally used on wallpapers. Pay particular attention to the edges of each strip and roll them several times after you have completed each section to make certain they do not curl back or lift up where strips meet edge to edge. Butt joints neatly; do not overlap them at all.

Foils and Mylars Like the vinyls, foils and mylars require a perfect surface. If your wall cannot be smoothed out by sanding, you may want to use a lining paper. Lining paper is blank wallcovering stock that is applied to prepared wall surfaces. It may or may not be able to be stripped. Lining paper prevents mildew and staining, improves adhesion, and creates a smoother surface. So that the seams of the liner and wallcovering do not coincide, the lining paper is usually hung horizontally. Use the same adhesive for the lining paper that you are using for your wallcovering and allow 36 hours drying time before doing anything else to the wall.

Apply the paste to the wall when applying either of these wallcovering types to prevent damaging their sensitive surfaces. Use a premixed vinyl adhesive and apply it ½ inch beyond the needed area using a medium ⅜-inch roller. Immediately hang the strip and work out the air bubbles with a roller rather than a smoothing brush. Do not use a seam roller. Since foil does not shrink or expand, any remaining bubbles should be punctured with a pin and pressed down. Rinse off excess adhesive immediately. After the adhesive has dried, wipe off water marks with a smooth cloth.

Flocks Flocked patterns are among the oldest and newest in existence. In recent years flocking has been added to almost any surface to which it will stick, but it still appears most widely in damask-type patterns that simulate cut velvet. Flocks need a little more preparation than the average wallcovering. In the first place, it is best to use a lining paper with flocks, as the raised flocking reflects extra light and betrays any unevenness of the wall. Second, they require the use of special, noncellulose paste, and this must be prevented from getting on the flocked surface as much as possible. For this reason the selvage on a flocked paper is retained until after a strip has been pasted. If paste does get on the surface, it must be sponged off and dried with a soft cloth immediately. Prolonged soaking of the paste on the back and overbrushing of the surface should also be avoided. This and other pertinent information and complete hanging instructions come with every purchase of flocked wallcovering.

Foils Foil patterns are a comparatively new development. Very thin sheets of gold, silver, and aluminum leaf, long used in the decoration of interiors and objects, led to the making of metallic papers from powder. These could be polished to a high shine, but foil coverings are gradually superseding most metallic-powder papers because of their superior brightness. Foils are actually a thin sheet of metal on a paper or cloth backing. In spite of their toughness they need to be hung (as do flocks) over a thoroughly dried-out lining paper, and each sheet of foil, after being pasted with a special adhesive, should be allowed from five to seven minutes for absorption and softening.

There are two methods of applying foil: by pasting the back of each strip, one at a time, or by applying the adhesive directly to the wall, preferably lined with paper, which a single strip will cover. Foil does not expand or shrink, so air pockets must be punctured and the material pressed against the wall to set it. If flocking is added to foil (currently a popular practice), the characteristics of each material must be taken into account when hanging the product. Whereas a seam roller of hard rubber could be used on foil (which is frequently mottled with color and encrusted with vinyl-impregnated substances), only a brush of soft natural bristles should be used to smooth any surface that is flocked.

Murals and Photographic Panels Murals and photographic panels present no difficulty in hanging; the planning of where and at what height they are to be hung is the biggest part of the job. In many museums and art galleries today, the paintings are hung lower than they formerly were. Presumably this gives a more contemporary and intimate look, as well as adding height to the room. But the furniture you use in conjunction with panels or a mural will determine at what level you want the interest centered. Just remember to relate any murals or panels to your furnishings as if they were pictures, and do not "sky" them. Since mural subjects are printed on plain-colored or textured precut strips that are much longer than the average height of a wall, it is simple, once you are sure, to cut the strips

to your own requirements.

As a general rule, the focal point of the scene should be approximately at eye level when you are seated. This means that the starting mark should be at or just slightly below the top of a furniture piece. Draw a level horizontal line at this point.

Determine the center point of the mural. This may be at the midpoint of the wall or at the center of some furniture piece. Drop the plumb line at this point. You will now measure to the left and to the right of this point to position the panels. If the mural has an even number of panels, simply measure full panel widths from the left and right of the point. Draw a new vertical at each 28-inch interval. For an odd number of panels, measure half the panel width (in this case 14 inches) to the right and left of the center point and draw two new verticals. This will be the position of the center strip. Continue to measure out full panel widths for the remaining panels. Hang the mural as you would any other wallcovering. The distance from the end of the mural panels to the corner of the wall will normally be filled in with the background panels furnished with the mural. Check that the width of these panels is the same as that of the mural panels prior to drawing the vertical guidelines.

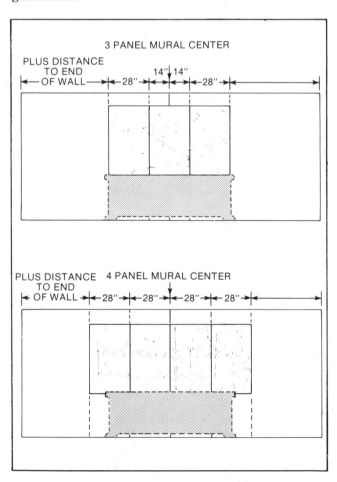

When locating a mural, start working from a center point.

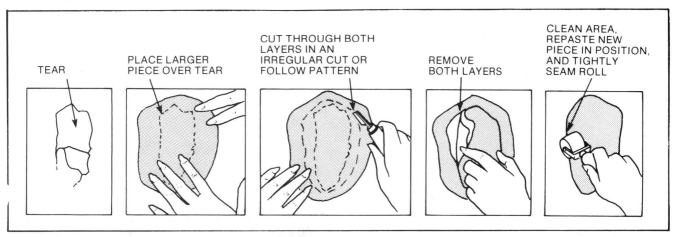

TEAR

PLACE LARGER PIECE OVER TEAR

CUT THROUGH BOTH LAYERS IN AN IRREGULAR CUT OR FOLLOW PATTERN

REMOVE BOTH LAYERS

CLEAN AREA, REPASTE NEW PIECE IN POSITION, AND TIGHTLY SEAM ROLL

Holes and tears in wallcovering can be repaired to make them barely noticeable.

Repairs and Care

You cannot afford to replace an entire strip of wallcovering every time a hole or tear appears. Instead, cut a piece of scrap wallcovering larger than the damaged area that will match the pattern. Place the piece over the tear and fasten with masking tape or hold it in position. With your razor knife, cut through both layers of the wallcovering around the tear. A cut that is irregular or follows the pattern will not be as noticeable as a square or circle. Use care when cutting on Sheetrock or dry construction wall. Remove both pieces and peel away the damaged old layer. The patch will now be a perfect fit. Clean the wall removing old, dry adhesive. Paste on the new piece and place in position. Roll around the edges with a seam roller after 10 or 15 minutes.

Loose Edges Pull a little bit of the strip away from the wall, apply the proper adhesive to the underside, press in place, and wipe off the excess adhesive. For vinyl you can use vinyl-to-vinyl adhesive or white glue; for paper, use white glue or library paste. Be careful not to soak the area with glue; just apply a thin even layer.

Bubbles and Blisters When an air bubble develops, cut a cross in its center with the razor knife and dampen the area with a sponge. Using the tip of the knife, lift up the sections of the cut and apply glue underneath with a brush. Push the paper back in place. When the paper dries, the edges should shrink back in place. In the case of foil wallcovering which does not shrink, simply puncture the bubble with a pin and push it in place.

Caring for Your New Wallcovering The one big plus of vinyl wallcovering is that it is easy to clean. If you have used vinyl, clean it with a damp cloth and a mild detergent. Do not use any abrasives that could scratch the surface. Heavy-duty kitchen and bath cleaners, providing they are nonabrasive, can be used for tough stains like pen and marker.

When washing a wall, wash from floor to ceiling, but rinse from ceiling to floor. This way you will not be washing down dirt onto an already rinsed area.

For nonwashable paper walls, minor marks may be removed by rubbing the area lightly with an artist's kneaded rubber eraser. By continually kneading it, you will be assured of a clean surface. Do not use a regular eraser as it will take off some of the paper fibers with the dirt. Some paper walls can be treated with a clear plastic coating to protect them from marks. Check with your wallcovering dealer for more information on plastic coating.

Flocks usually require no more than a touch-up with the soft brush of a vacuum cleaner. Go in one direction so the nap will lay properly. Some flocks are washable, but make sure yours is one of them before attempting to wash it.

Foils, for the most part, can be handled like vinyls. Again, avoid abrasives which could scratch the highly reflective surface of the foil.

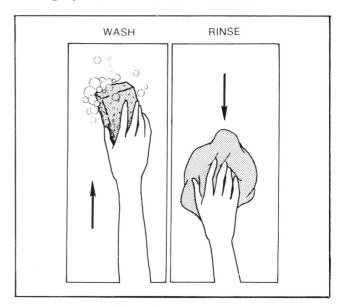

WASH   RINSE

Washing vinyl wallcovering.

How to Panel Your Walls

Paneling helps create beautiful walls in all types of rooms—walls suited to a variety of furnishings, cabinets, fixtures, and appliances. Whether for remodeling or new construction, paneling is simple to install because it is uniform in size, covers walls rapidly, is light but sturdy for handling, and matching moldings are readily available. And just as important, paneling provides years of beauty with little upkeep.

Even if you are not skilled at carpentry, paneling a wall or several rooms can produce results you can be proud of, while using such basic tools and materials as a saw, drill, hammer, tape measure, nail set, plumb line, plane or rasp, sandpaper, nails, and panel adhesive. In addition, you can choose paneling in accordance with your budget, your decorating ideas, and your room specifications. There are two types of paneling commonly used in homes: plywood and hardboard.

Plywood

Plywood panels come in a variety of hardwood and softwood finishes ranging from richly figured oak, mahogany, birch, and walnut to fir and pine, allowing a choice of decorative material to meet every taste and budget. They can be applied effectively to either traditional or modern interiors. One special appeal of plywood is that it allows you to decorate, utilizing woods that you might never be able to afford in the solid plank form. Since the core and back of plywood panels are cut from relatively inexpensive wood, a more stylish or elaborate wood can be used as a veneer without tremendously increasing the cost.

One outstanding advantage of plywood for interiors is the elimination of periodic patching of cracks. Plywood walls are kickproof, punctureproof, and crackproof. They are also resistant to warping, and have fair insulating and sound absorbing qualities. The only upkeep required is occasional waxing. Plywood thicknesses range from ¾ inch down to ⁵⁄₃₂ inch, but the ¼-inch-thick, 4-foot-wide, and 8-foot-long large panels are the most popular because they can be erected quickly and easily with ordinary hand tools.

There are three main types of plywood paneling with which you should be familiar. Real wood paneling has a thin slice of wood bonded to a plywood base and then finished. This type has the advantage of giving you the natural grain and color variations present in solid wood boards. With grain print paneling, the plywood base is first painted an opaque color. The grain and color of a more expensive wood is then printed on the painted surface. These are less expensive than the real wood veneers. This type is also available printed with material textures to simulate wallcoverings. In paper overlay paneling, a photographic copy is made of a desirable wood, scene, or texture and printed on thin paper. This paper is then glued to the plywood surface.

Selection of Panel Arrangement   There are many interesting ways to arrange panels in architecturally and decoratively correct designs. Many of these can be used on all the walls in a room; others are intended to create a point of interest or contrast in one part of the room only. In the latter cases the rest of the room may be paneled with full length plywood in natural finish or with less expensive or lower grade plywood, painted or papered. Plywood panels can also be used in combination with painted or papered plaster, glass, glass block, masonry, and other wall materials.

Plywood paneling adds a touch of elegance to this study area.

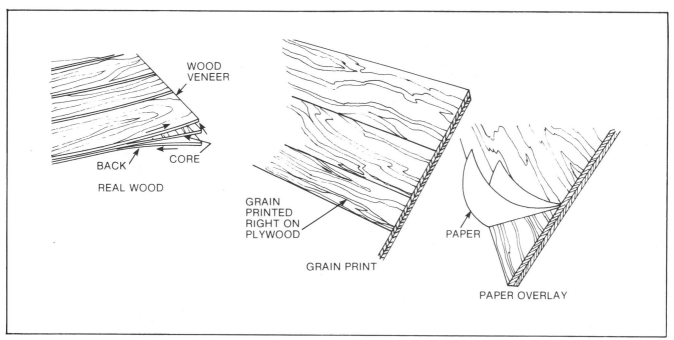

Three types of plywood paneling.

In choosing your panel arrangement, remember that it is best to start paneling at the openings, with vertical joints and then divide the plain space in an orderly pattern, placing the panels in a reasonably balanced horizontal or vertical arrangement. Where the width of the wall is 10 feet or less, panels may be run horizontally in two or three pieces, with the openings cut out. Place vertical joints at each side of the top of doors and at the top and bottom of window openings. If the width of the door or window opening is more than 4 feet, most designers do not hesitate to place panels horizontally. Remember, you can plan vertical arrangements to lend height and horizontal paneling to give breadth and sweep. Both can be combined in the same room with a pleasing effect. In certain woods, panels 9 or 10 feet long are available to solve special paneling problems.

A rough pencil drawing of walls to be paneled will help you design the best arrangement for the room. Always plan to let the joints between the panels follow the pattern set by the vertical joints at the openings. This helps to maintain a pleasing symmetrical design. Include locations of windows, doors, and other openings or obstructions on the drawing.

Estimating the Amount of Plywood Required

To estimate the number of panels required, measure the perimeter of the room. This is merely the total of the widths of each wall in the room. A conversion table has been included to help you figure the number of panels needed.

Although these kitchen walls appear to be finished in wallcovering, it is actually scenic paneling.

Plywood Panel Estimation	
Perimeter	Number of 4 x 8-foot panels needed*
20 feet	5
24 feet	6
28 feet	7
32 feet	8
36 feet	9
40 feet	10
44 feet	11
48 feet	12
52 feet	13
56 feet	14
60 feet	15
64 feet	16
68 feet	17
72 feet	18
92 feet	23

For a room with an 8-foot ceiling.

For example, if your room walls measured 14 feet + 14 feet + 16 feet + 16 feet, this would equal 60 feet or 15 panels required. To allow for areas such as windows, doors, and fireplaces, use the following deductions: door, ½ panel; window, ¼ panel; and fireplace, ½ panel. Assuming your room has two doors, two windows, and a fireplace, the actual number of panels would be 13 (15 panels minus 2 total deductions). If the perimeter of the room falls in between the figures in the table, use the next higher number to determine panels required. In fact, it is not a bad idea to have an extra panel on hand in case of miscuts. These figures are for rooms with 8-foot ceiling heights or less. For walls over 8 feet high, select a paneling which has V grooves and that will stack, allowing panel grooves to line up perfectly from floor to ceiling.

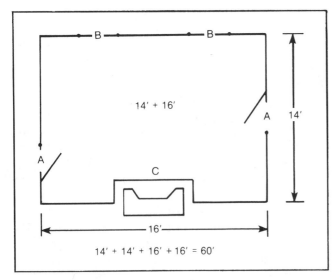

Computing the number of panels needed for the installation. Take deductions for the two doors, two windows, and fireplace.

For most wall paneling, ¼-inch plywood sheets are used. Of course, ⅜- and ¾-inch panels may be applied with good results, but they are more expensive. The latter thickness may be used as a partition without framing. For special designs, such as patterns made up of small panels—16- to 24-inch diamonds, squares, etc.—it is best to first sheathe the walls with 5/16-inch Plyscord, then apply the finish panels as desired.

Storing Plywood Paneling Panels should be stacked flat in a dry place prior to installation. Although prefinished plywood paneling is highly resistant to moisture, it is by no means waterproof and should not be installed or stored in areas where it will be subject to prolonged wetness. This includes storage in new plaster or masonry structures which retain considerable moisture. A room is considered relatively dry, and therefore suitable for plywood storage, if the humidity is between 40 and 50 percent.

The paneling should be conditioned to the room where it is to be installed at least 48 hours prior to the application. Either line up the panels vertically on edge against the wall or stack them on top of two full-length furring strips with wood blocks between panels to allow air to circulate.

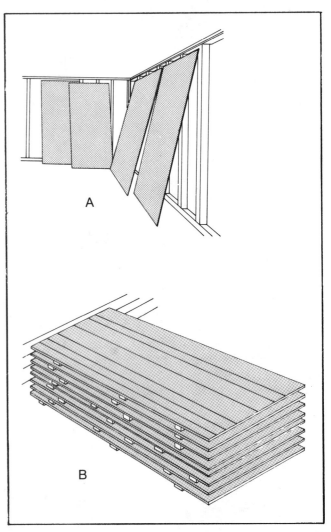

Condition the paneling by (A) standing upright or (B) stacking.

Erection of Paneling in New Construction
Whether new or old, the studs should be straight, dry, plumb, and true to assure a smooth, flat wall surface. If new framing is being installed, use only #1 Common, thoroughly dry, straight framing lumber of uniform width and thickness. Framing should be erected on 16-inch centers. Window and door frames should be furred out to equal the panel thickness so that the moldings will fit naturally. Where required, extra framing members should be installed to provide a nailing base for all edges of the panels. Nail vertical framing members at 4-foot intervals for additional support of panels, if needed, for every

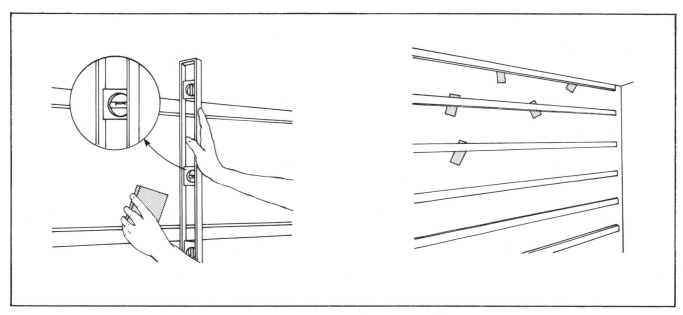

If the furring strips are not level, shim them out.

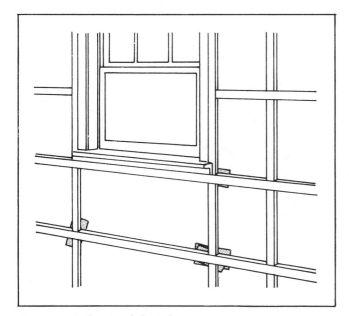

Fur out window and door frames.

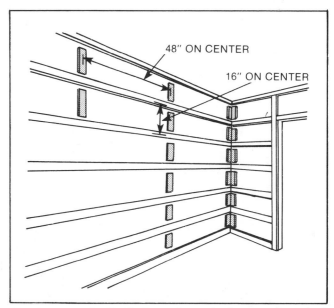

48″ ON CENTER

16″ ON CENTER

Furring may be flushed out through the use of vertical framing members spaced 4 feet apart.

panel edge and for every 4 feet of panel. If you are in doubt about the dryness of the framing lumber, apply fur strips (¼ inch thick, 2½ inches wide, and 4 feet long), with the grain running the short way over the face of the framing members. For studs spaced 16 inches on centers, use ¼-inch plywood; for studs placed 24 inches or more on centers, apply ¾-inch panels.

Begin by removing light fixtures, outlet and switch plates, and ceiling and floor molding from the walls. Molding can be taken off by driving the nails all the way through the strips with a nail set. Leaving molding on can result in a sloppy fitting job. Use a magnetic stud finder, which responds to the nails in the walls, to determine the location of the studs. This can also be accomplished by tapping

for a solid sound with a hammer or by probing with a nail. Check the stud spacing in several locations because it may not be uniform. At each stud location drop a chalked plumb line, hold straight, and snap. These will serve as nailing guides later on.

Plan the sequence of panels about the room so that the natural color variations form a pleasing pattern in complementary tones or in direct contrast. Hold each panel against the wall to see how it looks before you nail it. Number the backs of the panels to keep them in the correct order.

Here are three ways to start paneling, based on individual room problems:

1. For most interiors, it is practical to start from one corner and work around the room.

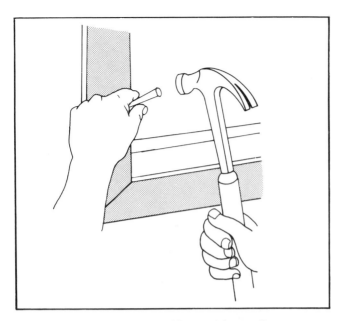

Drive nails through the molding with a nail set.

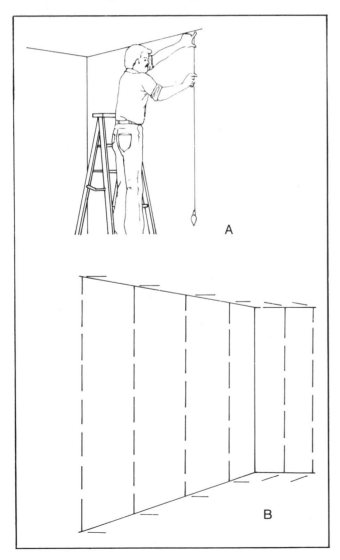

(A) Tack a plumb line at the ceiling and (B) snap lines at each stud location.

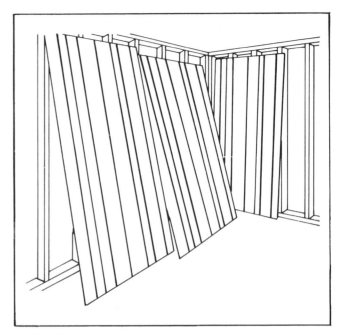

Arrange the panels in the proper order before applying them.

2. If the wall or room has a fireplace or picture window, you should start paneling on each side (if fireplace or window goes to ceiling) or at the center (if fireplace or window does not go to ceiling), and work to the right or left around the room.

3. If all the panels are the same width and window or door units are balanced across a wall area, start at the center of the wall and work both ways.

Again, do not be concerned about the natural variations in color as they will enhance the appearance of the room, as long as there is some symmetry of arrangement.

There are several tricks for laying out panels to reduce cutting as well as to achieve a pleasing pattern of joints. To avoid intricate fitting around windows and doors, start full panels on each side of the openings. On plain walls, it is best to start at the center so that fractional panels will be the same at each end. You can keep all joints vertical, the simplest arrangement, or use the tops and bottoms of windows as guidelines for horizontal joints.

Be sure that the panels are square with the adjacent wall (at corners) and ceiling before nailing. If the corner is not even, tap two finishing nails into two grooves at the top edge of the panel, just protruding through the back of the panel. Place the panel in the corner at a distance that can be spanned by your scribing compass. Using a carpenter's level, plumb the panel on the outer edge. When plumb, drive the nails partially into the stud or furring strip. Then, using your scribing compass, scribe a line from top to bottom. For a good line, use a china

Scribing a line for an irregular surface.

marking pencil. Cut the scribe line with a finishing saw. This method can also be used for corners with fireplaces, bricks, or stone.

Put the first panel in place and butt into the corner. The outer edge of the panel should fall on a stud line. Scribe to correct any irregularities. Use regular finishing nails, countersink the heads, and fill with a putty stick. Use a nail set to avoid damaging the panel's surface. Eliminate the need for countersinking by employing colored nails that match the paneling surface. Use 1-inch nails to apply paneling directly to studs or furring strips; use 1⅝-inch nails for applying over old walls. Space the nails 6 inches apart along all panel edges and 12 inches apart along intermediate studs.

Butt successive panels firmly against the first panel, but not forcefully. Keep the bottom of each wall panel about ¼ inch above the floor to allow space for the lever used to pry the panel tightly against the ceiling. As the panels go up, keep checking them for plumbness. Shim out the studs or fill hollows of the framing. Keep a level handy for tru-

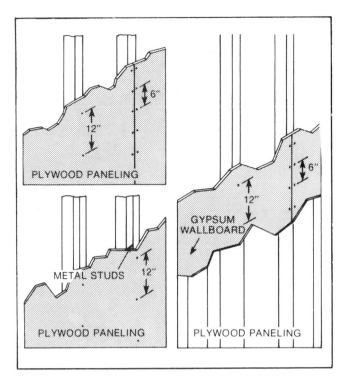

Spacing of nails for applying plywood paneling to different surfaces.

Use shims to keep the panels ¼ inch off the floor.

ing up and down (vertical position). Molding will take care of the irregular meeting with floor and ceiling. When nailing, start along one edge of the panel and work across the width so as to avoid bulges.

When cutting plywood with a handsaw or on a table saw, the plywood should be cut with the good face up. If you are using a portable electric handsaw, either circular or saber, cut the plywood with the good face down. If you are using a radial saw, cut the plywood with the good face up for crosscuts and miters, and down for ripping. With a handsaw or on a table saw, permit only the teeth of the blade to protrude through the work. For added insurance, apply

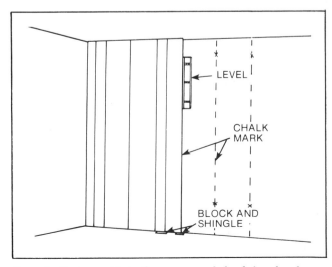

Butt the first panel into the corner and check for plumbness.

Work with the face side of the paneling up when using a handsaw, and with the face side down when using a portable power saw.

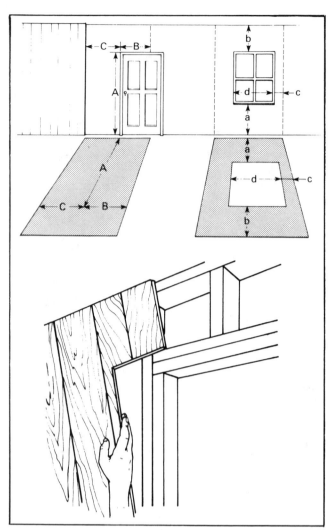

Measuring and installing window and door cutouts.

a strip of tape along the cutting line to reduce potential splintering. For smooth cuts, use blades that have teeth with no set and that are hollow ground. Special small-toothed blades are available for cutting plywood.

Measure from the edge of the last panel installed to the edge of the untrimmed door or window opening. Mark this on the panel to be cut. Next, measure the height of the door or window and mark this on the panel. Cut to fit, remembering the side from which to saw the panel. If it is possible, your cutout panels should meet at the middle area above and below your window or above your door. The panel will be easier to work with than if the cut is out of the middle of the panel. If you must cut out of the middle of the panel, be sure your measurements are correct. Drill a ¾-inch hole (from face side) at the corners of your measurements to give you a turning corner if using a keyhole or saber saw for the cutting. In a remodeling job, you should fur out the window and door frames to equal the panel thickness, so that your window and door moldings will fit naturally. To cut around fireplaces, use a compass and scribe around the bricks and other irregularities; trim along the scribed line. For pipes and posts, box them in with small pieces of paneling and molding. This same technique can be used for deep-set windows and for the center beam in basement ceilings. Mark electrical outlets as described in the solid wood paneling chapter.

Installing with Adhesive   The application of plywood with panel adhesive is widely employed. Its use largely eliminates the need for brads or nails and the resulting concealment of their heads. Generally, the adhesive comes ready to use in a tube with a plastic nozzle. This tube fits into almost any

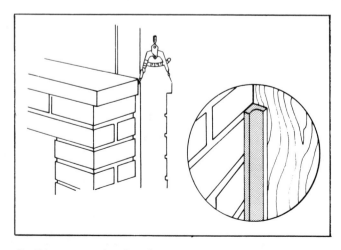

Scribing around a fireplace.

caulking gun, and the panel adhesive comes out of the nozzle as a heavy bead. We have included a table to help you to determine how much adhesive will be needed for the job. This table gives the bead length in feet as related to bead size diameter in inches.

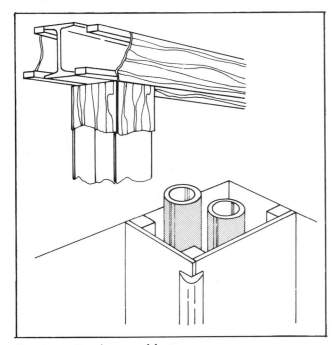

Box in posts, pipes, and beams.

Paneling Adhesive					
Volume	Bead Size in Diameter				
	⅛″	³⁄₁₆″	¼″	⁵⁄₁₆″	⅜″
	Lineal Feet of Extruded Adhesive (length)				
Small Cartridge (11 fluid ounces)	135	60	34	21½	15
Large Cartridge (29 fluid ounces)	355	158	89	57	39
1 Gallon (128 fluid ounces)	1,569	697	392	251	174

In round figures, 1000 feet of adhesive bead will require:

⅔ gallon at ⅛-inch diameter bead
2½ gallons at ¼-inch diameter bead
5¾ gallons at ⅜-inch diameter bead

If the wall is in good condition, smooth and true, the adhesive can be applied directly to the back of the panel all around the edges in intermittent beads about 3 inches long and spaced about 3 inches apart. Keep the adhesive at least ¼ inch from the edges of the panel and be sure that it is continuous at the corners and around openings for electrical outlets and switches. Additional adhesive should be applied to the back of the panel in horizontal lines of intermittent beads spaced approximately 12 to 16 inches apart. Once the adhesive is applied, the panel

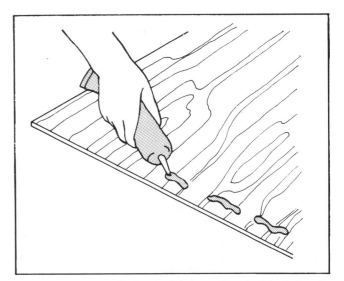

Apply adhesive to the back of the paneling in 3-inch beads spaced about 3 inches apart.

may be pressed against the wall. Make sure the wall is clean and dry. It may be moved as much as is required for satisfactory adjustment. To make this easier, drive three or four small finishing nails about half their length through the panel near the top edge. The panel can then be pulled away from the wall at the bottom with the nails acting as a hinge. After any adjustment has been made, a rubber mallet or a hammer and padded block should be used on the face of the panel to assure good adhesion between panel and wall. Drive in the finishing nails at the top of the panel. An equal number of nails should be driven in along the bottom edge. These nails will be covered by the molding. If any butt edges bow out, drive a finishing nail through a small block of wood and through the joint. Remove it after 24 hours. Never attempt to apply adhesives on plaster walls in poor condition, with flaking paint or wallpaper that is not tightly glued. If the

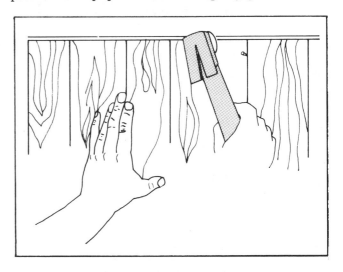

Finishing nails driven partially into the panel act as a hinge.

Use a hammer and a padded block to assure good adhesion between the panel and the wall.

plaster seems hard and firm and does not crumble when you drive a nail into it, it is probably safe for adhesives.

There is an alternate method of installation on existing wall surfaces that provides you with an outstanding paneling job. Where the existing wall is plaster, gypsum board, or another smooth backing, a trowel grade construction adhesive or tileboard adhesive may be used. In this case, trowel the mastic over the back surface of the panels utilizing a trowel with notches approximately $\frac{3}{16}$ inch deep, $\frac{3}{16}$ inch wide, on $\frac{5}{16}$ inch centers, unless otherwise specified by the manufacturer.

Adhesives may also be used on furring strips and open studs. It is applied directly to each furring strip or stud in continuous or intermittent beads. Before applying the panel adhesive to open studs, it is a good idea to inspect all studs for low spots with a chalk line or straightedge. Mark those studs that have one or more low spots. (To locate studs after paneling is up, put a chalk mark on the floor at the base of each stud.) Draw a plumb line on the stud

that is 4 feet from the corner. Where studs are straight, apply a ¼-inch high bead of panel adhesive. Where studs have one or more low spots, apply a ⅜-inch bead. On the studs at the edges of the paneling, apply the adhesive inside the plumb line to keep the adhesive from squeezing out at the edges. On the other studs, follow the plumb line.

To install paneling on metal studs, proceed in the same manner; however, be sure that the adhesive manufacturer recommends it for metal studs. Employ self-tapping screws rather than nails to hold panels in place at the top and bottom.

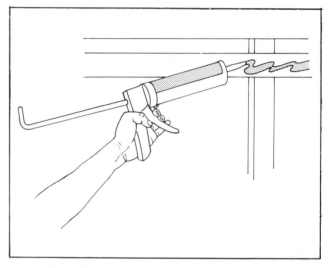

Apply the adhesive bead to furring strips or open studs.

A word of caution about prefinished panels: handle them with care. Should the surface scratch, repair it according to the instructions under the section on care. To avoid soiling the panels, apply the finish to the trim and molding before installation. Most of the larger companies make hardwood moldings that will harmonize with their various types of plywood. Some sell moldings that are already finished to match, while others sell special stains that will enable you to blend the trim in with the finished wall later on. Some companies also make veneered metal moldings with a matching wood facing to conceal exposed plywood edges and to finish off inside or outside corners.

Erection over Old Plaster and Dry Wall
Where existing walls are in good condition, you can put the panels right over the old surface and nail through it into the studs. On dry walls (wallboard and plasterboard), you can find the studs by prying off the baseboard molding and noting the points where the panels have been nailed on. When nailing, make sure to go through the wall material into the studs beneath with small finishing nails or brads, which will be countersunk, and into the plate and sill with heavier nails where moldings will cover the area.

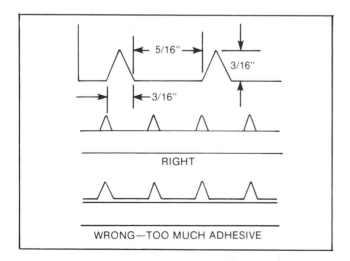

Proper spacing for trowel notches.

On walls that are badly out of line or where the plaster is cracked, you may have to put up a light framework of 1-by-2-inch furring strips to cover the irregularities and ensure a true vertical surface. Be sure to level with shims. One-quarter-inch three-ply fir-plywood strips 2½ inches wide are ideal for this purpose, except in cases where paneling is used with recess joints. With such joints, it is proper to use strips that match the face of a hardwood panel. Apply the furring horizontally across the studs, nailing it into the studs. Then fit on vertical furring wherever it is required to provide a nailing surface behind all panel edges. Shim all the furring plumb and true, and nail through the plaster into the studs every 16 inches with 8d cut-steel nails or resin-coated nails.

Erection over Cement and Masonry Walls
In such installation, furring strips are a necessity because of the inherent dampness resulting from seepage or condensation. They allow air to circulate behind the panels. The strips can be attached by drilling holes and using wood plugs or expansion shields. An alternate method is to attach the strips with cement nails. If needed, coat the walls with a waterproofing paint. Particularly if the walls are underground, a vapor barrier should be used. Four-mil thick polyethylene sheets, overlapped 3 inches at seams, make an effective barrier. If you prefer to use insulation, make sure you install it with the vapor barrier facing you. Painting the back side of the panels with a sealer, such as shellac, will also preserve them. To keep condensation under control after the paneling is up, consider purchasing a dehumidifier.

Installing Plywood Wall Planks Plywood plank panels are 8 feet long by 16¼ inches wide and they go up without furring strips—over wallpaper, plaster, sheathing, or bare studs. They are grooved on the long edges in a special design that makes the installation of plank paneling the quickest of all plywood walls. The material is held by special clips that you nail into the wall or studs. Follow the manufacturer's directions.

Wainscots Wainscot paneling goes only partway up the wall, usually extending no more than 3 or 4 feet above the floor. The top section is then painted, papered, or decorated with some other wall material. This type of treatment is frequently seen in kitchens and dining areas. Cap molding is applied along the top edge when using paint or paper, and batten molding is used if the upper section will also be done in paneling.

Rooms with High Ceilings One way to deal with the problem of high ceilings is wainscoting. Work up to the 8-foot level, and then use another wall treatment up to the ceiling line. Panels can also

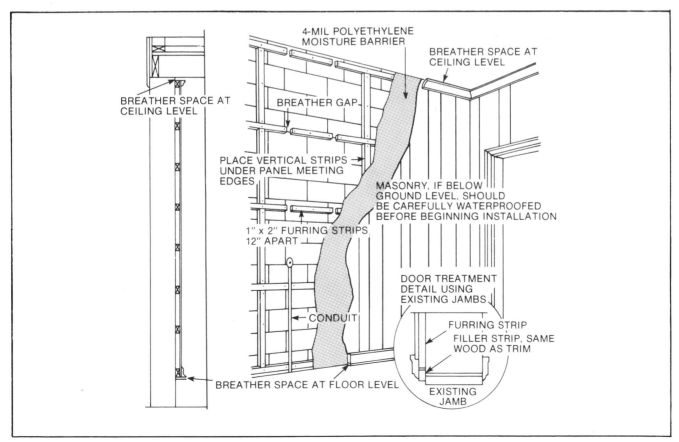

Installing plywood panels on below ground masonry walls.

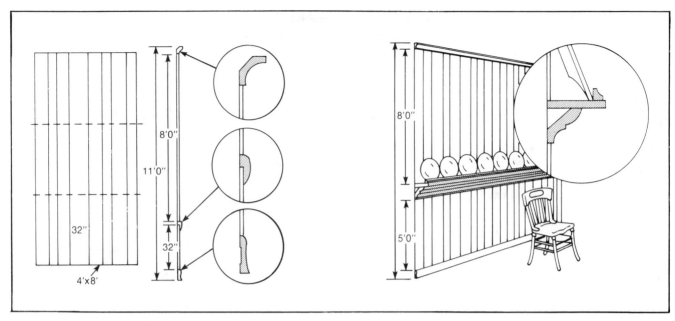

Two possible arrangements for paneling walls that are over 8 feet high.

be stacked one on top of another using molding at the seams. Locate moldings so that the wall looks balanced. Use a short panel as a wainscot, then top with a full-size panel.

Paneling can also be stacked horizontally. This is one of the simplest solutions if you do not mind the strong horizontal lines. If you are more daring, you could install the paneling diagonally or in a herringbone pattern. Cutting can be done at a 45-degree or 60-degree angle. Make sure, however, you measure and plan out the wall carefully before starting to cut. For the best results, locate one complete V at the center of the room.

Care Most veneered panels can be cleaned with a damp cloth or with special liquid wood conditioners for the real wood veneers. Stubborn marks such as crayon may be cleaned with mild soap. Rinse and allow to dry. Do not use abrasive cleaners or steel wool pads which could scratch the surface. A vacuum cleaner can be used to clean strongly textured panels.

A surface scratch can usually be removed through waxing. Major scratches may either be repaired using a putty stick or, if serious, might require refinishing.

In bright rooms, pictures should be hung so that

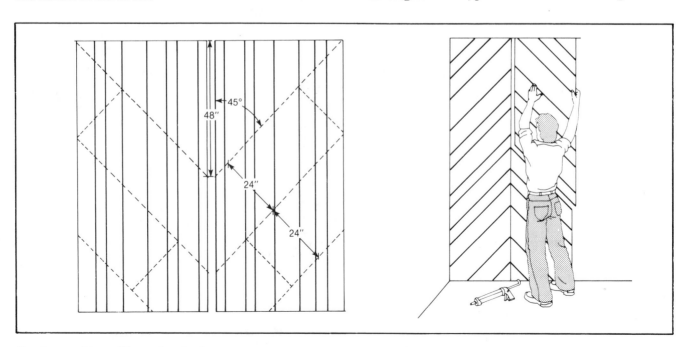

Cutting and installing a herringbone pattern.

they stand out approximately ½ inch from the wall. This will allow light behind the picture and will keep any light-caused fading uniform.

Low humidity can adversely affect any wood product just as extreme dampness can. If the paneled room becomes very dry during the winter, consider adding a humidifier.

Most plywood panels will wipe clean.

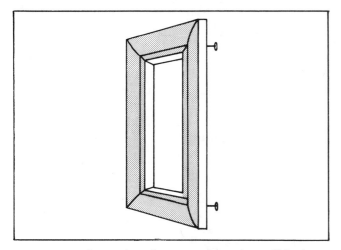

Pictures can be made to hang out from the wall by hammering nails partially into the back of the frame.

Hardboard

Hardboard, the generic name for Masonite, is specially manufactured for use as prefinished paneling. It is specifically treated for resistance to stains, scrubbing, and moisture. It is also highly resistant to dents, mars, and scuffs. In most cases, the material is prefinished in wood grains such as

Attractive curved wall formed with hardboard paneling.

walnut, cherry, birch, oak, teak, and pecan, and in a variety of shades. It may be smooth-surfaced or random-grooved. Unusual textures not available in plywood, such as brick and stone, can be found in hardboard form. In addition there are the decorative and work-saving plastic-surfaced hardboards which resist water, stains, and household chemicals exceptionally well. A typical surface consists of baked-on plastic. Most hardboard is sufficiently dense and moisture-resistant for use in bathrooms, kitchens, and laundry rooms. However since the panels are made of wood fibers, they will expand somewhat in high moisture conditions. The variety of finishes and sizes is extensive. Finishes include rich-looking wood grains, exceptional marble reproductions, plain colors, speckled colors, simulated tile, lace prints, wallpaper textures, and murals. Vinyl-clad panels are also available in decorative and wood-grain finishes.

Preparations Measure for the panels you will need. It always helps to measure and remeasure the entire area to be paneled, and then plot these measurements to scale on graph paper. Make a plan view and also a layout of each wall showing fixtures, electrical outlets, and other details. Also indicate each type of molding and where it will be installed. Remember, panels come in 4 by 8-foot sheets and most moldings in 8-foot lengths. Refer to the table on plywood paneling to estimate the number of panels needed.

Use ¼- and ⁵⁄₁₆-inch hardboards over open framing. All panel edges should be backed by a stud, furring strip, or solid wall. Studs or framing members should be spaced no more than 16 inches on center. Use ¼- or ⁵⁄₁₆-inch board thicknesses for structural wall members. Hardboards that are ⅛ and ³⁄₁₆ inch thick should be applied over solid backing. Quarter-inch-thick boards may be applied directly over studding or stripping not over 16 inches on center.

For most new construction, it is recommended that 1 by 3-inch furring strips be glued to the studs. To bring out the face of the strips to a level plane, shim the furring with ordinary shingles driven between the wall and the strip. Glue or nail the shingles in place. When furring over masonry, apply the strips with a construction-type adhesive. Another alternative is to attach the strips with masonry nails, and then anchor them with nails and mastic. Arrange the hardboard panels around the room in the desired sequence, standing them against the wall. Do not slide the panels over each other. The panels should be allowed to stand in this manner for 48 hours prior to installation.

To prepare an existing solid wall for the board, remove all wallcovering, scaly paint, or dirt. Then remove such fixtures as the lavatory, toilet tank, and wall-hung accessories. Next mark an accurate starting point for your panel. For a wainscot effect, this line is usually 48 inches above the floor. In floor-to-ceiling work, use a level to establish the horizontal joints and a plumb bob to mark the location of the vertical joints.

A third way to handle masonry walls is to construct a free-standing wall of 2x3 or 2x4 studs, 16 inches on center. This frame is then attached to the ceiling and floor.

Plan for a gap of ¼ inch between the paneling and the floor to be covered later by base trim. Allow ³⁄₁₆ inch between panels to make provision for a ¹⁄₁₆-inch expansion space between each panel edge and the inside of the divider molding. Never force the panels into metal molding grooves and always leave a little space for expansion.

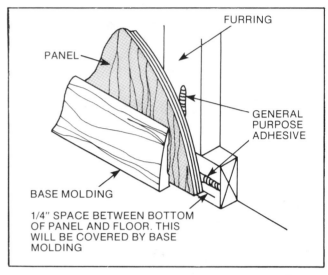

Leave a ¼-inch gap between the floor and the bottom edge of the paneling.

It is important that the work be done in the proper sequence. Some of the metal moldings must be installed before the wall panels are fitted and placed in position, but it is convenient to install others as the job progresses. Remember that the moldings overlap the panel edges, therefore do not fit molding over the last two panel edges until the panel has been positioned properly. To cut the metal molding, use a hacksaw and miter box, and file off the rough edges after cutting. The molding has wide flanges through which nails are driven; panels conceal nailheads. Where moldings meet in a corner, flanges

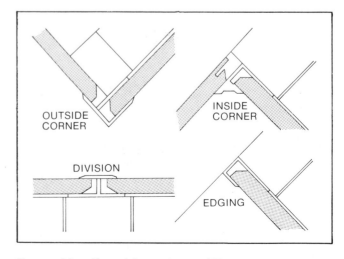

Types of hardboard fastening moldings.

must be cut back so they do not overlap. Some panels have special corner moldings available. With planning, you can make a decorative feature out of the molding lines.

Installation   Begin at an inside corner; nail cap molding along the line marking the top of the wainscot (use miter joints in corners). Also nail an inside corner molding in the corner, extending from the top of the base trim to the bottom of the exposed flange of the cap molding. It will be necessary to cut away a little of the wall flange where it overlaps the cap molding. Next, check the corner to see if it is straight and plumb. If not, it will be necessary to scribe the edge of the panel and trim it to conform to the corner. Fit, but do not install, the divider molding for the exposed vertical edge of the panel (remove part of wall flange where it overlaps the cap molding).

For full-height panels, start at an inside corner and nail a strip of inside corner molding extending from the top of the base trim to the ceiling. Next, install a piece of cap molding along the wall/ceiling intersection. Mark a plumb line the desired distance from the corner to locate the first vertical joint. To compensate for unevenness or lack of plumb in the adjoining wall, place the first panel in perfectly plumb position so that the distance between the panel and the wall area to be scribed can be spanned by your scribing compass. Rule a scribing line and cut the panel with a coping saw if an uneven cut is required.

Cut the hardboard panels with a fine-tooth crosscut saw, eight to twelve teeth per inch, held at a low angle. All cutting should be done with the panel face up. If a portable electric saw is used, the panels should be face side down when cut. With a power circular saw, use a crosscut or combination blade. A metal-cutting type blade, seven or eight teeth per square inch, should be used with a band saw. Sand

the rough edges. Try the panel for size, lining it up with a guide line. It may be best to measure the height of each panel individually as the ceiling may be irregular. To get added protection against buckling of the boards with expansion, bevel the edges that fit into moldings. Trim each edge down with a plane or sandpaper until it moves freely into the molding. Bevel on the back side with an ordinary plane held at a 45-degree angle.

Apply the adhesive to the back of the panel, not to the wall. Lay the panel on a padded support and spread the adhesive with a notched spreader. A trowel with $\frac{3}{16}$-inch notches is recommended. For a waterproof seal, put adhesive or caulking bead in the molding grooves. Remove any adhesive that gets on the face of the sheet at this point with a soft cloth and a solvent designated by the manufacturer.

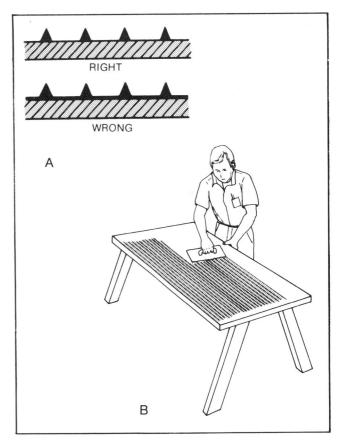

(A) Determining and (B) spreading the correct amount of adhesive on the back of a hardboard panel.

Slip the panel into position and press it tightly against the wall. Next, apply adhesive in the groove of one of the divider moldings (previously fitted and set aside) and slip it into place along the panel edge. Check to see that the divider is plumb, then fasten that edge of the panel by nailing through the exposed flange. Return to the panel and press it firmly against the backing, working from the center toward the edges. Repeat this after 20 minutes to en-

Plumbing the first corner panel.

sure good contact. Also, remove any excess adhesive from the finished surface as soon as possible. Be sure the room is well ventilated to dissipate the solvent, and do not permit smoking or an open flame in the room while solvent is being used.

Although this method is losing popularity, hardboard panels can also be nailed into place. Start nailing from the center of the panel out toward the edges. This will prevent waviness. Space nails 8 inches apart on intermediate studs and 4 to 6 inches apart along panel edges. Keep nails approximately ½ inch from the panel edges. The nails must be long enough to penetrate the framing members.

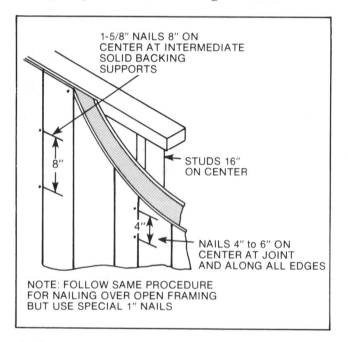

Applying hardboard paneling by the nailing method.

Subsequent panels should be installed in sequence. To put a prefitted panel into place when only one side is open (i.e., surrounded by molding on three edges), slip one end of the panel into its molding strip. Bow out the center until the other end slips into the molding. Release the curve and slide the panel edge into position behind the third molding. Panels around doors and windows should be fitted loosely to allow for expansion.

Before fastening these panels to the wall, make sure they are plumb by using a level of sufficient length to give you an accurate reading. The slightest irregularity in fit between panels can cause them to get out of plumb. It is easy to adjust panels if each one is plumbed.

The panels should be in only moderate contact with each other. They should never be butted tightly together. V-grooved panels are beveled at the edges, and when lightly butted they form a full-depth groove. To prevent wall show-through at joints, darken the area behind the joint with a black felt-tip pen. Other hardboards adapt to a variety of joint treatments: rounded edges; bull-nose wooden inserts; wood, plastic, or metal moldings; battens; and lap joints. For hardboards that are patterned so that the edges blend into the overall pattern of the board when they are butted together, leave a space between panels the thickness of a matchbook cover. Where joints are exposed, a beveled or rounded edge may be used. Inside corners may be covered with cove molding or gently butted. Actually, to give the job a finished look, use moldings around windows and doors, in corners, along baseboards, and, where applicable, over joints.

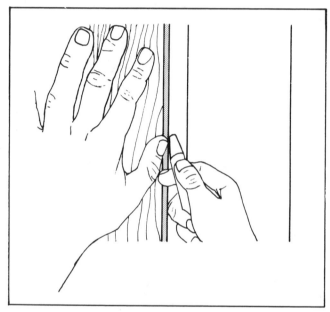

Color in joint areas with a marker.

A cap molding to run along the top of wainscots can be made adjustable by nailing through the slots in the flange instead of the holes. The slots are saw cuts. Place the nail at the end of the slot (do not drive it too tightly) to permit the molding to slide under the molding head. Move the molding ¼ inch to the side until after the panel is in position. Then, place a wood block along the side and gently tap the molding into place with the flange covering the panel edge. Short lengths of cap molding can be attached to the panel edge with adhesive or caulking before the panel is put into place on the wall. Be sure to put adhesive on the back of the molding as well as the back of the panel. If necessary, temporary bracing may be used to hold the panels into position until the adhesive has set. Usually, this is not necessary, as the moldings will prevent the panels from moving.

Bath Installations   Before starting to panel walls around bathtubs or showers, turn off the water supply and line the tub with protective material to avoid scratches. Then remove towel bars, soap dishes, faucets, and other accessories.

The joints between the tub and paneling must be made permanently watertight. First, bend flexible tub molding to fit closely against the tub/wall intersection. Clean this area carefully to ensure a good bond, then caulk the back of the tub molding and nail it in place. Seal the nailheads with caulking.

It is best to start with the panel at the faucet end of the tub. Depending on whether you want a wainscot or a full wall installation, follow the general procedures given previously. Consider, however, if the best procedure will be to start by installing a molding at the inside corner and work both ways or to start at the outside corner and work progressively around the tub. Horizontal joints must not be installed in shower areas.

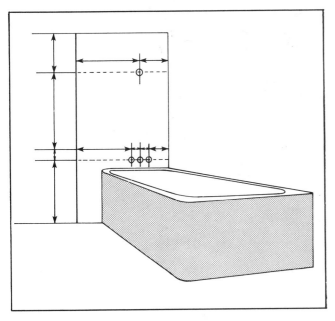

Constructing a paper template for bathroom paneling installations.

Using heavy paper, make a template showing the location of faucets, valves, shower head, and other features. After double checking the template for accuracy, transfer the pattern to a panel that has already been cut to fit the wall. To make the cutouts, drill a starter hole, then use a keyhole saw to cut the opening. When the panel has been fitted properly, apply adhesive to the panel back, fill the tub molding groove and other moldings with caulking for a waterproof seal, and press the panel into position. When continuing with the installation, be sure that the panel edges, joints, and moldings are well sealed with caulking for a watertight installation.

Care The best rule on care for hardboard paneling is to follow the manufacturer's directions. Usually, simple dusting will be sufficient to keep the panels looking like new. If washing becomes necessary, use a mild, nonabrasive soap that will not affect the finish. Some manufacturer's recommend using a low-luster furniture polish or liquid wax. If you do decide to use one of these products, try it on an inconspicuous spot first. To protect the finish of any hardboard paneling, never apply masking tape or pressure-sensitive stickers to the surface.

Perforated Hardboard Perforated hardboard, or pegboard, is a very versatile material. In addition to being a most attractive wall material, perforated hardboard may be a permanent solution to the problem of using your walls for more than just places to hang pretty pictures. There is a wide variety of fixtures available at most hardware stores that makes it possible to use walls for many different purposes.

When applying perforated hardboard over studding, cut the panels into widths that equal a multiple of the center-to-center stud spacing. On a wall where 2-by-4-inch studs are located on 16-inch centers, for instance, cut the hardboard to widths of 16, 32, 48 inches, and so forth. Try to plan the width and placement so that you will not have narrow pieces at the wall ends. Since no furring is required over bare studs, place the perforated panels so that the edges fall on stud center lines and nail them directly to each stud, using 3d finishing nails spaced about 8 inches apart. Countersink the nailheads and fill the holes with plastic wood or wood putty. As an alternate method, panels may also be glued to studs, using contact or panel adhesive. Install them as directed for regular hardboard.

When perforated hardboard is applied over an existing wall surface, the installation of furring is necessary since the holes in the paneling must have space behind them so that the fixtures can be inserted. If you plan to panel an entire wall this way, it is a good idea to place a row of 1-by-2-inch strips along the bottom of the wall, end to end, after removing the old baseboard. Repeat the process at the ceiling. Then, nail vertical furring at the edges of the wall from floor to ceiling. Finally, placing them horizontally again, nail the strips from end to end 2, 4, and 6 feet above the floor. Once the furring strips have been applied, the perforated panels can be fastened in the same way to the studs, except that the strips are glued or nailed.

When cutting a panel, make sure that the saw blade does not pass through a row of perforations, since the resulting edge is most difficult to conceal. There are two other methods of making a joint in addition to butting the two sides together. The first is to nail a molding over the joint. The second is to plane a 45-degree bevel along the meeting edges before the panels are installed. The groove that results wherever the panels meet can then be filled with wood putty or spackle and sanded smooth before finishing with paint. This will result in an invisible joint.

Solid Wood Planks and Boards

Despite the popularity of sheet paneling materials, none can compare with the beauty and warmth of solid wood boards or planks. The solid woods, however, are more expensive and may not be practical for remodeling jobs conducted on a tight budget. For informal treatment, knotty pine, redwood, whitepocket Douglas fir, sound wormy chestnut, and pecky cypress may be used to cover one or more sides of a room. These woods may be finished natural or stained and varnished. In addition, there are such desirable hardwoods as red oak, pecan, elm, walnut, white oak, and cherry also available for wall paneling. Most types of paneling come in thicknesses from ⅜ to ¾ inch; widths vary from 4 to 8 inches, lengths from 3 to 10 feet.

Vertical redwood planks produce a warm, cozy atmosphere in this study.

When planning a wood-paneled room, remember that if you wish to accent a wall, use boards of random widths; subdue it by the use of equal-width boards. Small rooms can be given the illusion of increased size by applying the paneling horizontally. Of course, paneling can be applied vertically, horizontally, diagonally, or in combined directions.

Solid wood is subject to shrinkage and swelling, even though kiln-dried. After delivery, therefore, stack the lumber inside the house at a temperature as close to room temperature as possible. The paneling should never be stored where it will be exposed to weather or to excessive moisture. The building or room in which the wood planking is to be installed

should be completely closed in and dry before installation begins. Masonry and other work involving moisture should be completed and dried. A vapor barrier such as polyethylene plastic sheeting (4 mils thick) should be provided behind paneling where any danger of moisture penetration exists. This is a requirement on outside walls and on all concrete or masonry walls. If insulation is to be used, apply the barrier between the insulation and the paneling. A waterproof sealant applied to masonry foundation walls will reduce the amount of moisture coming in from the outside. If you are working with damp masonry walls, another good idea is to apply a wood preservative containing pentachlorophenol to the back of each panel. This will protect the paneling against moisture, mildew, fungus, and termites and other insects.

Before doing any installation, lay out the boards on the floor adjacent to the installation wall. With solid wood, the wood grain from board to board will never match exactly. This is part of its natural beauty. Arrange the most attractive combination of widths, lengths, grain patterns, and shades of color. Then install the boards in the selected sequence. Use shorter pieces at the top and bottom of the wall area, where more than two pieces are required for wall height. Stagger the end joints to form a pleasing pattern on the wall, and avoid positioning two or more end joints near each other. Vary the widths to enhance the random effect. For best contrast, use narrow planks adjacent to wider ones. There are several types of groove patterns available. The channel rustic patterns provide strong vertical accents with bold shadow lines, while the bevel-edged tongue-and-groove and shiplap patterns offer the more subtle V-groove effect. Where no accent line at all is desired, square-edged adaptations are used to create tight, flush joints. Most patterns may be installed either vertically or horizontally; the choice is yours.

Estimating Materials To figure out how many boards you will need for the installation, determine the square footage—width times height of each wall and add the figures together. Subtract the footage of open areas such as windows. Convert your measurements to board feet and linear feet by multiplying by the conversion factors in the given table. For example paneling a 50 square foot area with 10-inch board means you would need 54.5 board feet (50 x

1.09) or 60 linear feet (50 x 1⅕). Allow at least 5 to 10 percent for waste and 15 percent for diagonal paneling.

Board and Linear Foot Conversions			
Lumber Width	Board Foot Conversion	⅜-inch Paneling Only	Linear Foot Conversion
4″	1.24	1.19	3
6″	1.15	1.12	2
8″	1.11	1.09	1½
10″	1.09	(wider lumber not available)	1⅕
12″	1.07		1

Installation Techniques Except where the walls are fairly even and in good to excellent shape, most vertical applications over plaster or similar walls require the use of 1 x 2 or 1 x 3 furring strips. These are installed (nailed or glued) horizontally on 16- or 24-inch centers. Make sure the wood is dry. Green wood can warp and ruin your project. Additional strips must be nailed around doors, windows, and other openings. Where the wall is uneven or wavy, wooden wedges or shims should be used behind the furring strips to bring them into an even line. Insert thin shims—one on top of the other—from opposite sides of the strip and tap them in with a hammer until the strip is even. A small nail will hold them in place.

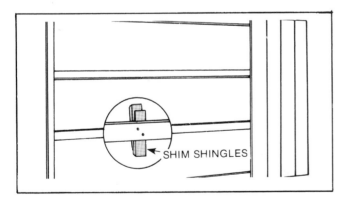

Use shims, one on top of the other, to level out furring strips.

Begin at an inside corner, working from left to right if you are right-handed, and vice versa if you are left-handed. Keep the tongue edges facing the direction of work progression. Trial-fit the first board, making sure that it is plumb or perpendicular with the floor. You can use a level or plumb bob (by snapping a chalk line on the wall) for this purpose. If the variation is less than ½ inch, the excess can be planed or sanded down. If it is greater than ½ inch, the board should be scribed. To do this, place

the board in a plumb position an inch or so from the corner. Carefully tack it in place. Run the compass down the length of the corner, and it will transfer the wall's variations to the plank or board. This waste area can then be cut off, and a perfect fit will result.

On furring strips, nail the top and bottom of the board in place; then blind-nail through the tongue every 16 or 24 inches depending on your strip spacing. For installing the boards directly to the wall, face-nail the top and bottom and every two feet—approximately ¾ inch from the corner—angling to penetrate the stud. You can locate studs in the wall by tapping (a studded area produces a solid sound) or by using a magnetic stud finder. Use 8d nails for ¾-inch boards when face nailing, and 6d nails when blind-nailing. Use proportionately smaller nails for thinner panelings. In humid locations, employ galvanized nails that will not rust or corrode. Special paneling nails are also available that are colored to match the paneling. Do not hit the panel surface with the hammer. Instead, leave them sticking out approximately ⅛ inch and use a nail set to drive them in the rest of the way. Set the nails 1/32 inch below the panel surface and fill the resulting holes with putty stick or filler. Be careful with oil-base fillers as they can stain the wood.

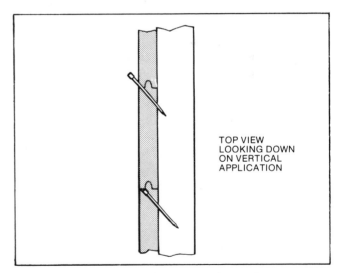

TOP VIEW LOOKING DOWN ON VERTICAL APPLICATION

Angle nails so that they penetrate the studs.

Fit other boards as you work, checking for plumbness and for tongue-and-groove fit. Tap them into place with a hammer and tapping block, then nail. Any joints should be made over a furring strip.

Prior to removing outlet and switch plate covers, turn off the current to the particular outlet or switch from the main box. To locate an outlet cutout on a panel, place the panel against the wall and, with a padded block over the approximate location of the outlet, tap it soundly with a hammer. The outlet box will indent the back side of the panel. Another

Countersink nailheads and fill with putty stick.

method is to chalk the edge of the outlet box and strike the face of the board several times with the heel of your hand to transfer the image. Drill small pilot holes from the back (larger holes from the finish side) and saw the outlet hole from the front side of the panel with a saber or keyhole saw. After the cutout has been made and the panel board installed, advance the receptacles flush with the panel surface by replacing the holding screws with longer ones, slipping pieces of electrician's loom behind as backing. Be sure that the loom is cut long enough to compress properly as the screws are tightened.

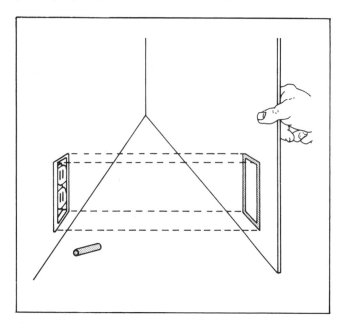

Chalk outlet boxes and tap to transfer outline to the back of the plank.

At outside corners, make 45-degree miter cuts on the board edges using a table saw. These boards can also be butted together by removing the tongue-and-groove sections with a handsaw. To end at an inside corner, it is usually necessary to trim the board in order to get it into place. With a block plane, angle the board's edge slightly with the widest part of the angle toward the wall. This way the board will be easy to position, while still giving you a good tight corner.

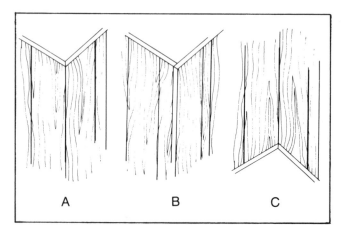

Constructing (A) inside miter, (B) outside butt, and (C) outside miter corners for vertical planks.

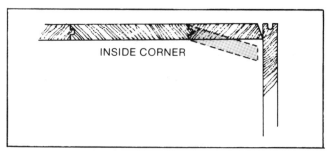

Trim the last board to fit into the corner.

Fit the solid paneling as close as possible around the untrimmed door opening thickness, allowing for a little natural expansion or contraction that could occur. The door, window, base, and ceiling trim should be removed before starting the job. Fur out window and door frames to equal the thickness of the furring strips plus thickness of the paneling. To give the job a finished look, use molding around windows and doors, along the floor and ceiling, and wherever else applicable.

In new work, wood paneling may be nailed to studs or furring in the same manner as plywood. A right-handed worker will prefer facing the tongues to the right and working from left to right, starting with a length nailed to a corner studding or furring. The boards that fill the space to the next stud are then laid out and cut to the proper length, the preceding one being used as a template to make sure that all are the same length. Each tongue should be fitted tightly into its groove by being rapped smartly with a hammer insulated by a tongued scrap of the wood. The boards between those anchored to studs can be secured to the top plate near the ceiling and to the shoe close to the floor. Warped lengths should be discarded. If possible, use only full-length pieces that extend from floor to ceiling, except where the wall is masked by bookshelves or other built-ins. Corners must be solid, which will usually require ripping at least one board for its full length to take off the tongue. The top of the paneling can be finished with a suitable cove or crown molding.

Horizontal Applications When solid wood paneling is to be applied horizontally on an existing wall that is reasonably sound and true, furring strips are not usually required. Once the trim has been removed and the studs located, the boards are nailed through the existing wall material into the studs. If the old wall surface is masonry, in poor condition, or not true, furring strips should be installed in the same manner as vertical solid paneling except that strips should run vertically rather than horizontally. Shim the strips to obtain a true nailing surface. Remember to nail furring around all openings as well. Inside corners are formed by butting the panel units flush with the other walls. Outside corners can also be butted, or they can be mitered at an angle a little greater than 45 degrees which is necessary for a good fit. If random widths are employed, boards on adjacent walls should be well matched and accurately aligned. When nailing the boards, be sure to install them so that the tongue edge is out. This will permit you to blind-nail through their tongues. Drive the nails in at an angle

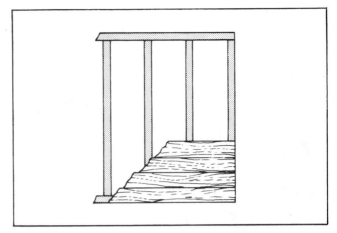

Start horizontal planks at the base of the wall.

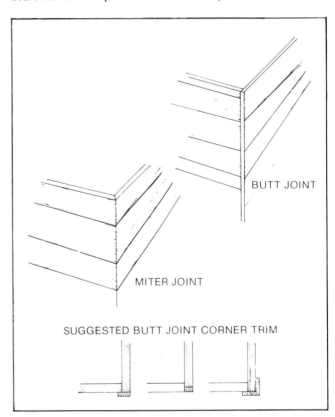

BUTT JOINT

MITER JOINT

SUGGESTED BUTT JOINT CORNER TRIM

Miter- or butt-join outside corners of horizontal planks.

so they come out the back of each board behind the tongue. The nailheads, of course, will be hidden in the groove of the next board. At the top of the wall, be sure to leave an expansion space of about ¼ inch. A molding will cover it.

Diagonal Applications Diagonal paneling installations are more often than not confined to one wall of a room and usually employ tongue-and-groove paneling. Recall that you will need 15 percent more material than for a standard vertical installation. If necessary, apply furring strips vertically as was recommended for horizontal applications. Start paneling at an inside corner, keeping the tongue edge facing the work direction.

Horizontal redwood planks bring the beauty of nature into any room.

Diagonal redwood accent wall.

Arrange the first three boards flat on the floor with the tongue edges up. Fit the tongue-and-groove sections together as they would appear when installed. Using a carpenter's square, mark a 45-degree miter cut across all three boards. Saw and then trial-fit. After any ragged edges have been sanded smooth, face-nail the corner piece and blind-nail the rest at each end and at the intersecting furring strips. To butt board ends in the middle of a wall, trim the edges square or miter cut. Joints such as these should fall over the stud or furring strip so that they can be nailed in place.

Adhesives for Solid Wood Paneling The ⅜-inch solid board paneling may be applied directly over sound, even walls using a paneling adhesive or mastic. Ask your building-supply dealer for advice concerning the types and brands available.

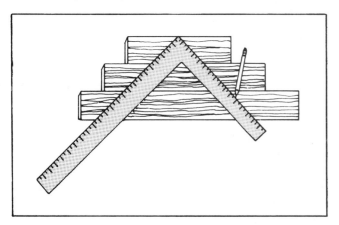

Miter cut through the first three boards in diagonal applications.

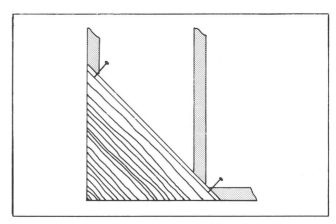

Blind-nail diagonal planks at intersecting furring strips.

As in nailing, make sure the first panel is aligned vertically at the corner of the room. After fit is assured, use a putty knife to apply daubs of adhesive to the back of the panel. These should be about the size of a half dollar, at least ½ inch thick and spaced 18 inches apart near both edges of the panel. Place the panel in position, and press it firmly to even out the adhesive and assure a tight bond. Succeeding panels are treated the same: placed close to the previous panel, pressed into place, and then slid tightly against it.

Another method is to apply the adhesive with a caulking gun. Follow the manufacturer's instructions as to setting time. Make sure you apply a line of adhesive around any cutouts or openings. You may still want to face-nail the top and bottom of the board to furring for added stability. These nails will be concealed later by the molding.

For masonry walls, attach and shim out furring strips as previously mentioned. Apply the panel adhesive to the furring and press the panels into place. When gluing the boards, be sure to install them so that the tongue edge is out. At the top of the wall, be sure to leave an expansion space of about ¼ inch. A cove or crown molding will cover it.

Finishing Solid Wood Paneling While most plywood and hardboard panels are prefinished, solid wood usually requires finishing. Varnishes form durable and attractive finishes for interior wood surfaces such as wood paneling and trim. They seal the wood, forming tough, transparent films that will withstand frequent scrubbing and hard use; and they are available in flat, semigloss or satin, and gloss finishes. Most varnishes are easily scratched, and the marks are difficult to conceal without redoing the entire surface. Polyurethane and epoxy varnishes are notable for durability and high resistance to stains, abrasions, acids, alkalies, solvents, strong cleaners, fuels, alcohol, and chemicals. Adequate ventilation should be provided as protection from flammable vapors when these varnishes are being applied.

Shellac and lacquer finishes are similar to those of most varnishes and are easy to repair or recoat. They apply easily, dry fast, and are also useful as sealers and clear finishes under varnish for wood surfaces. The first coat should be thinned as recommended on the container. After it is applied, the surface should be sanded very lightly and then finished with one or more undiluted coats. Two coats will give a fair sheen, and three a high gloss.

Liquid and paste waxes are used on interior sur-faces. They provide a soft, luxurious finish to wood and are especially effective on trim. Waxes should be applied to smooth surfaces with a soft cloth and rubbed with the grain. Brushes should be used to apply liquid waxes to raw-textured wood. Wax fin-ishes can be washed with a mild household deter-gent, followed by rinsing with a clean, damp cloth. A wax finish is not desirable if a different type of finish may be used later because wax is difficult to remove.

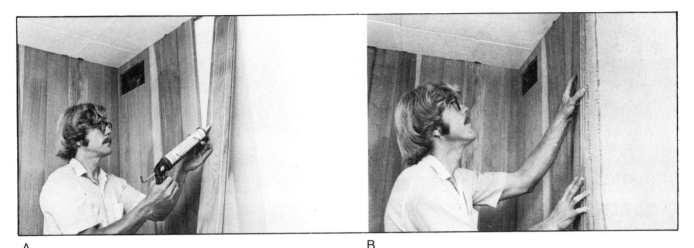

A   B

(A) Apply adhesive to the plank, (B) press into place, and tap planks against each other to assure a tight fit.

Common Finishes for Solid Wood Paneling		
Type of Finish	**Finishing Materials Used**	**Method of Finishing**
Light natural	1. Two coats satin-finish lacquer or varnish 2. Good quality paste wax	Apply coat of satin finish; steel-wool when dry. Apply second coat of lacquer or varnish; steel-wool the second coat and then wax.
Pickled effect	1. White plywood sealer or undercoater 2. Two coats satin-finish lacquer or varnish 3. Good quality paste wax	The white plywood sealer should be thinned 10 to 20 percent with mineral spirits or turpentine. Allow to set three to five minutes. Rub into the pores and wipe clean, not leaving a painted effect. Allow to dry 24 hours. Lightly sand with fine sandpaper. Apply one coat lacquer or varnish; when dry, steel-wool. Apply second coat. Steel-wool when dry; then wax.
Slightly pickled effect	1. Natural paste wood filler 2. White plywood sealer 3. Two coats satin-finish lacquer or varnish 4. Good quality paste wax	Apply a coat of natural paste wood filler mixed with about 10 percent of white plywood sealer. Rub well into the pores and wipe off thoroughly. Let dry for 24 hours. Apply first coat of lacquer or varnish. When dry, steel-wool and dust off. Apply second coat, steel-wool, and dust off when dry; then wax.
Blond effect	1. White plywood sealer 2. Two coats satin-finish lacquer or varnish 3. Good quality paste wax	The white plywood sealer should be thinned 10 to 20 percent with mineral spirits or turpentine. Allow to set three to five minutes. Rub into the pores and wipe clean, not leaving a painted effect. Allow to dry 24 hours. Lightly sand with fine sandpaper. Apply one coat lacquer or varnish; when dry, steel-wool. Apply second coat. Steel-wool when dry; then wax.

Common Finishes for Solid Wood Paneling (Continued)

Type of Finish	Finishing Materials Used	Method of Finishing
Full flush finish	1. Wood filler (shade desired) 2. Two coats satin-finish lacquer or varnish 3. Good quality paste wax	Apply paste wood filler of desired shade, rub well into wood, and clean off. Let dry 24 hours, and apply first coat of lacquer or varnish. When dry, steel-wool and dust off; then apply second coat. Steel-wool and dust off when dry; then wax.
Oil-stained effect	1. Clear or white plywood sealer (tinted) 2. Two coats satin-finish lacquer or varnish 3. Good quality paste wax	Apply oil stain made of white or clear plywood sealer thinned about 20 percent with turpentine or mineral spirits and tinted with colors-in-oil to the desired tone. (Use white sealer as base for gray and pastel and clear sealer for oak, maple, and darker shades.) Let this coat set a few minutes; then rub well into pores and wipe off thoroughly. Let dry for 24 hours. Apply first coat of lacquer or varnish. Steel-wool when dry, dust off, and apply second coat; steel-wool, dust off when dry, and wax.
Colonial or Cape Cod effect	1. Clear plywood sealer (tinted) 2. Pure white shellac 3. Good quality paste wax	Thin the clear plywood sealer 10 to 20 percent with mineral spirits or turpentine. Thoroughly mix in approximately ½ ounce (by weight) burnt umber in oil and approximately 3½ ounces (by weight) raw umber in oil to the gallon. Brush on and wipe off in three to five minutes, depending upon the intensity of color desired. Let dry overnight and apply a thin coat of pure white shellac. Sandpaper dry and wax thoroughly.
Modern gray effect	1. White plywood sealer or undercoater tinted 2. Two coats satin-finish lacquer or varnish 3. Good quality paste wax	First tint the white plywood sealer with a little lamp-black ground in pure linseed oil and a touch of light chrome yellow to equal the shade on the panel. The tinted white plywood sealer should be thinned 10 to 20 percent with turpentine or mineral spirits. Allow to set three to five minutes. Rub into pores and wipe clean, not leaving a painted effect. Allow to dry 24 hours. Sand lightly with fine sandpaper. Apply a coat of lacquer or varnish; steel-wool when dry. Apply a second coat of lacquer or varnish; steel-wool the second coat; then wax.
Sheraton mahogany effect	1. Stain, medium mahogany color 2. Light mahogany paste filler 3. Pure white shellac 4. Two or three coats good quality varnish	Apply medium mahogany-color stain evenly. When dry, sand lightly with fine sandpaper. Apply light mahogany paste filler following manufacturer's directions. Sand lightly. Apply thin coat of pure white shellac. Apply coat of good quality varnish and sandpaper lightly when dry. Apply second coat of varnish. Sand with very fine sandpaper. Rub with rubbing compound.
Light Sheraton effect	1. Extralight mahogany filler 2. Two coats satin-finish lacquer or varnish 3. Good quality paste wax	Apply extralight mahogany paste filler, following manufacturer's directions on the can. Let dry overnight. Lightly sand with fine sandpaper. Apply coat of satin lacquer or varnish; steel-wool when dry. Apply second coat of lacquer or varnish; steel-wool when dry; then wax.

Note: It is a good idea to use a filler on open-pored woods. On walnut, use standard walnut wood filler; on mahogany, use standard light or dark mahogany wood filler; for antique oak effect on oak, korina, elm, ash, etc., use antique oak wood filler; for natural finish, use natural wood filler or tint it to the desired shade with colors in oil. For flush finish with white pores, use special white wood filler.

Other Materials for Your Walls

In the previous chapters we discussed the three most common ways to dress up your walls: paint, wallcoverings, and paneling. But there are several more materials you can use to create interesting and attractive effects. These include imitation stone and brick, ceramic tile, mirror tile, and wood strip. Also included in this chapter is a section on moldings, which can be used to dress up virtually any of the wall materials mentioned in this book. Molding is not only used at the top and bottom of walls, but also on the space in between to achieve various decorative designs.

Imitation Brick and Stone

For interior use, simulated plastic bricks and stones are inexpensive, easy to install, and, in most cases, look like the real thing. But in addition to their decorative value, these textured wall surfaces can be installed without having to add bracing to the floor or a step to the foundation, which would be necessary with ordinary brick or stone because of the weight.

Imitation bricks and stones are made of various plastic materials: styrene, urethane, and rigid vinyl are the most common. Some are fire resistant and may be used as fascias for fireplaces. All false bricks and stones are highly durable and come in a wide variety of colors and styles. Some are sold in sheet form, while others are installed individually in white, gray, tan, or black mastic. They can even be obtained already applied to ¼- and ¾-inch plywood. Select whatever brand appears the most realistic to you.

Installing Imitation Brick and Stone   Start at the top of the wall and work down. Make a level horizontal starting line for yourself. Do not rely on the ceiling line being straight; it usually is not. When you reach the bottom of the wall, bricks or stones may have to be cut to fit. Make a second plumb line, this time a vertical one, at your starting corner. Spread a 1/16-inch coat of mortar on the wall. Do not work an area larger than 2 by 4 feet at a time. With certain types, the back of the brick must be buttered with mortar as well. Using a twisting motion, slide the brick or stone into place, squeezing the mortar up into the cracks. Try to keep even spacing between

A

B

Some imitation (A) brick and (B) stone are fireproof and suitable for use as fireplace fascias.

the pieces. As you work, smooth the joint lines with a brush. After the mortar has dried, finish the job with one or two coats of sealer.

The brick or stone may need to be cut to fit the bottom row or to go around obstructions. Mark the line, make a shallow cut with a hacksaw, and snap. For delicate cuts, use a tile cutter.

There are several ways to work corners. Some manufacturers make special corner pieces. These wrap right around the corner and are the easiest

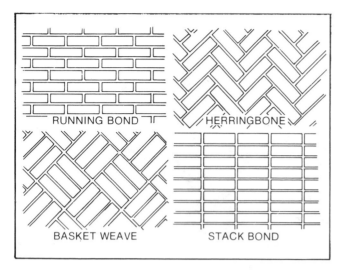

Possible wall installation patterns using imitation brick.

A

Apply a thin coat of mortar to the wall.

B

(A) Smooth joint lines with a brush. (B) When the mortar has dried, apply two coats of sealer.

Move the brick or stone into place with a slight twisting motion.

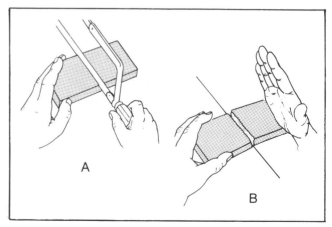

To cut imitation brick and stone, (A) make a shallow cut with a hacksaw and (B) snap.

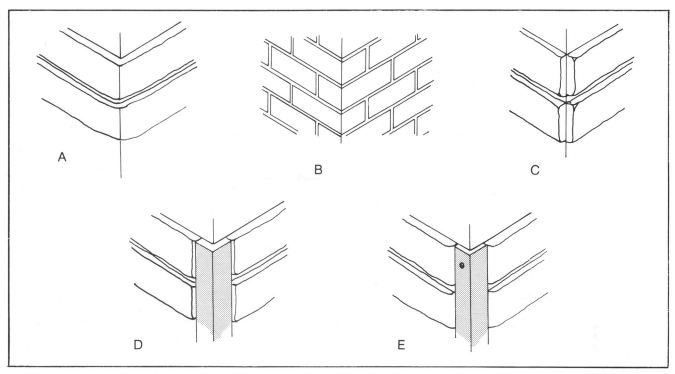

Various corner treatments: (A) prefabricated corner pieces, (B) mitered, (C) flush, (D) wood molding, and (E) metal angle.

way to tackle the problem. If corner pieces are not available with the type of brick you are using, miter the bricks using a hacksaw and fill in the joint with a mixture of one part sealer to three parts brick dust. Other alternatives include bringing the pieces flush to the corner on both sides or filling in the center line with a wood molding or metal angle.

Ceramic Tile

Though more expensive than many of the wall materials, tile offers the advantages of great beauty and durability. Tile is virtually waterproof, cleans easily, and will not fade, scratch, burn or stain. Under the right conditions, tile applications have lasted many years. You can do an entire room in tile, just an accent wall, or use it to frame windows, doors, and fireplaces.

Imitation brick can be used to form arches around unsightly basement posts.

Tile walls are durable and long-lasting.

Types Tile offers variety in color, size, and shape. Tile itself is simply pieces of clay that have been fired at high temperatures to produce high hardnesses. The most popular tile type is glazed wall tile. It is available in the widest range of colors and comes in square, rectangle, hexagon, octagon, and curved Moorish shapes. The most common wall tiles are the 4½-inch and the 6-inch squares. The glazed surface can have a gloss, crystalline, or matte finish. Ceramic mosaic tile comes in 1-inch and 2-inch squares and is often attached to a mesh or paper backing. These are frequently seen in bathroom installations. Quarry tile is heavy-duty floor tile, but it may also be applied to walls. Most come in earth tones like red, chocolate, and beige. Thin 1½-inch bricks, known as pavers, are also suitable for covering walls.

Preparing the Walls Tile can be installed over plaster, gypsum board, wood, paneling, paint, and other tile. Just make sure that the surface is in good repair and is clean. Painted walls should be sanded to roughen the surface. Wallcoverings cannot support the weight of tile and should be removed.

Estimating Tile Amount Find the perimeter of the room, and then multiply it by the ceiling height. For an 8 by 10-foot room with a 7-foot ceiling this would be: 8′ + 8′ + 10′ + 10′ = 36′; 36′ × 7′ = 252 square feet. (For one wall application, just find the area of that wall.) Now multiply this figure by the number of tiles needed to cover one square foot. Using 6-inch square tile, for example, you will need four tiles per square foot or 252 square feet × 4 for a total of 1,008 tiles. Deduct the footage of doors and other areas that will not be covered. Always purchase a little more tile than you will need and buy all the tile from the same dye lot to assure a good color match.

To make the installation, you will need the following tools: notched or smooth trowel, glass cutter, sponge, nippers, carpenter's level, chalk line, pencil, a few finishing nails, and rubber gloves. You will also need thinner or solvent and adhesive. One gallon of adhesive should cover approximately 45 square feet of wall area. Unless the tile is pregrouted, you will also need grout. The silicon type is best because it resists mold and mildew.

Installation Start tiling at the floor line in most rooms. The exception is in the bath where the tile should begin at the tub line. Measure the height of one tile from the floor (or one tile plus ¼ inch for a bath). Snap a horizontal chalk line around the room at this point. Remember to allow for space if you will be installing a ceramic molding. Next snap a center vertical line on the starting wall. Using the center line as a joint line, lay out the first row of tile working from both sides of the line to the

corners. Do not forget to include space for the grout line. Most tiles, however, have tabs to keep them evenly spaced. If the last tiles in the row will be smaller than a half tile, you must readjust the center line. Tiles smaller than this are difficult to cut and detract from the finished wall.

Apply the adhesive for the first row of tile that falls directly above the chalk line. Do not work more than 3 or 4 feet at a time. You may want to tack up a furring strip below the line to support the tile. Apply the first row of tile. Press tiles firmly into the adhesive using a slight twisting motion. When you reach the end of the row, you may need to cut a tile. Score the tile surface with a glass cutter. Place a finishing nail directly under the scored line, and apply pressure on both sides of the line to make the break. Professional tile cutters can sometimes be rented from tile dealers.

Apply adhesive to the wall with a notched trowel.

Remove the furring strip and go back and install the bottom row of tile. In most cases, it will be necessary to trim the tile because of an uneven floor line; take small nips until the desired amount is removed. Leave one tile off the end on the third row up. As you continue upward, leave one more tile off the next row than off the previous one to create a staircase arrangement. This allows for easier adjustment if the lines start going crooked. Continue tiling until the wall is complete. Let openings for switches and outlets. To fit tiles around pipes and other obstructions, there are two ways to proceed. The first is to break the tile in half, nip out the center, and then fit the tile back together around the

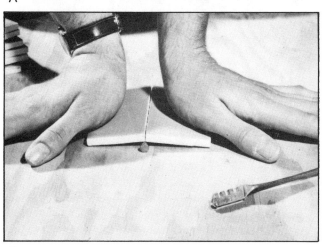

(A) Installing and (B) cutting ceramic tile.

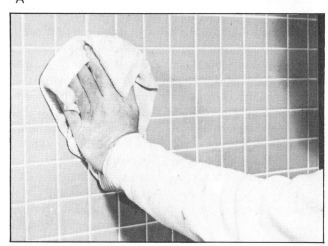

(A) Apply the grout, wait a few minutes, and (B) wipe it off the tile face.

pipe. If the pipe can be detached, use the second method which involves cutting out the tile center and slipping it over the pipe.

After all the tiles are in place, remove any adhesive on the tile face with solvent. Allow the tiles to set undisturbed for a day. Then apply the grout. Since many grouts are caustic, wear gloves while making the application. Apply the grout with a sponge using upward and back-and-forth strokes to force the grout into the cracks. Grout 25 to 30 square feet at a time. Pregrouted tile will only need attention around the sheet edges. After a few minutes, wipe the grout off the tile face. Tap the seams flat with the handle of a toothbrush. After the grout has set, buff any film remaining and seal the grout.

Mirror Tile

Mirror tile is a versatile and exciting way to cover walls. The addition of a mirrored wall will make rooms seem bigger and brighter. Mirror tiles are

Bevel-edged mirror tiles open up a small dining room.

easy to install, relatively inexpensive, and easy to clean. Plus, they are available in a wide variety of colors and patterns. There are the traditional clear squares; copper, pink, blue, and green pastels; swirl, vein, bamboo, and plaid patterns; and geometric designs. Most are available with either a square or a beveled edge. Silk-screened mirror graphics, mirror strips, and elegant mirror arches are other choices.

Installing Mirror Tiles In order to determine the number of tiles required, find the area (length times width) of the wall to be covered. This will give you the square footage. Since each tile is 12 by 12 inches, or equal to one square foot, the number of tiles needed is equivalent to the square footage. For example on an 8 by 10-foot wall: 8 feet × 10 feet = 80 square feet or 80 mirror tiles. The tools necessary to do the job include the following: level or straightedge, plumb line (chalked string with a weight on the end), tape measure, mounting tape, tile cutter, felt-tip pen, and mirror cleaner.

Make sure the wall surface is clean and dry. Find the center point of the wall and snap a vertical chalk line. Now mark the point that is midway up the wall and snap a horizontal chalk line. You have now divided the room into four equal quarters. Place tiles face side down, peel one side of the protective backing from the mounting tape, and apply the tape to the four corners of the tile. Do not touch the surface of the tape or you will reduce its bonding abilities. Use a double thickness of tape to level out uneven wall areas. Remove the other side of the tape backing. Place the first tile where the vertical and horizontal lines meet in one of the quarters. Work outward in horizontal rows until all full tiles are in position.

To work around doorways, switches, and other obstructions, you must cut the tile. Measure the distances from the obstruction to the full tiles already in place. With the mirror side up, mark the measurements on the tile with a felt-tip pen. Holding the cutter firmly in your hand, cut moving downward along a metal straightedge. Do not stop or change the pressure on the cutter; this will result in an uneven cut. Hold the tile at the bottom on both sides of the cut line and snap. To complete the wall, add mirrored outlet and switch covers.

Installing Graphics Mirror graphics are produced in a multitude of designs suitable for any decor. The graphics are 36 by 24-inch pictures composed of six mirror tiles. Measure and mark off the area to be covered by the graphic. Make sure your lines are plumb. Apply the mounting tape to the tiles as previously described. Lay the tiles face up so they form the intended picture. Remove the other side of the backing and install the tiles in sequence.

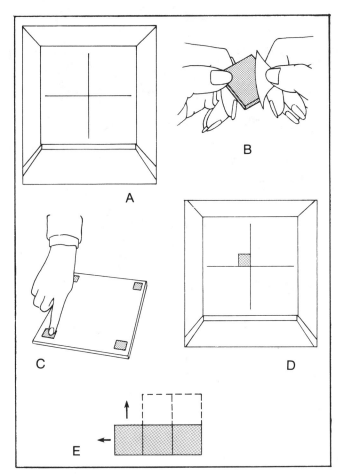

Steps in installing mirror tile: (A) Line off the wall, (B) peel off one side of protective backing from the tape, and (C) apply the tape to the back side of the tile; (D) place the first tile at the intersection and (E) work upward and outward from that point.

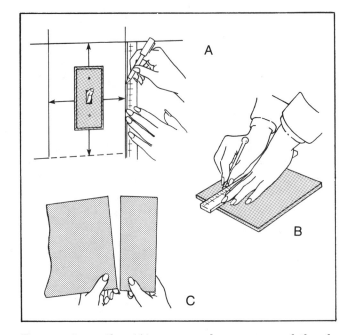

To cut mirror tiles, (A) measure the area around the obstruction, (B) score the tile with a glass cutter, and (C) snap apart.

Mirror graphics are attractive alone or in combination with a mirrored wall.

Installing Strips   Mirror strips can be used to cover walls or doors, as backsplashes, or as free-standing screens. Both plain and bevel-edged types are produced. Measure and mark where each strip will go. Try to have as many strips as possible fall over a stud. For beveled strips, mark the top and bottom screw holes; for plain strips, mark where the mounting clips will be placed.

Mirror strips offer an alternative to the tiles, giving long, unbroken vertical lines.

To install beveled strips over studs, place the felt sleeve over the enclosed screws, and screw them through the holes in the strips. Toggle bolts should be used in place of screws in plaster and wallboard applications. Do not overtighten the screw or bolt, or you will crack the mirror. To complete the job, place felt washers on the decorative buttons and screw the buttons into the screw or bolt head. To apply plain strips, install top and bottom mounting clips, insert the mirror, and tighten.

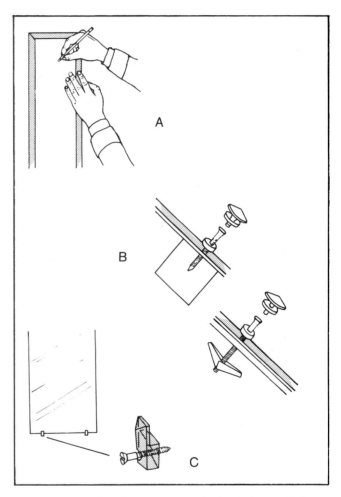

(A) To install beveled strips, mark the holes and (B) attach with screws or toggle bolts. (C) For plain strips, use mounting clips.

Installing Arches   Measure and mark the wall where the mirror clips will be located. There are two possible clip arrangements. For the first, center one clip at the top and one on each side of the mirror, and place two at the bottom, out toward the corners. In the second arrangement, two clips are again placed at the bottom, but none at the top. Instead, two clips are placed on both sides. Divide the height of the arch into thirds, and place clips at the one-third and two-third marks. Use screws for attaching to studs and toggle bolts for plaster and wallboard. Install the arches.

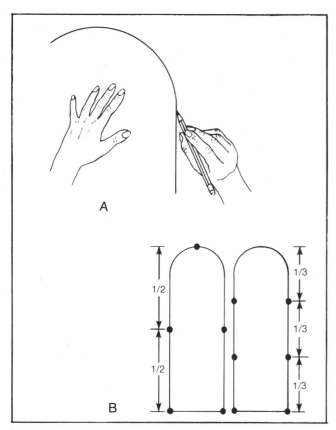

(A) Measure and mark where the arches will go. (B) There are two possible clip arrangements that can be used.

nail holes and joint areas because the strips will cover them, but brightly colored paint may show through. Give the walls a primer coat of brown or some other color paint that will blend in with the wood strips.

Installing Wood Strips   Strips may be cut with sharp shears or a utility knife. When using a knife, cut along a metal straightedge. For pieces under 5 inches long, cover the back with masking tape to keep them from splitting. Do not remove the tape; apply the adhesive directly over it. When making vertical cuts, put a strip of masking tape on the face of the panel along the cutting line.

Apply the strips with any type of nonwater-based paneling adhesive; a waterproof mastic should be used for bathroom installations. You will need approximately 1½ to 2 tubes of adhesive for every package of wood strip used. Start applying wood strips at the base of the wall. If you must start at the top, use staples to hold the strips in place until the adhesive dries. Cut the adhesive nozzle for a ⅛-inch bead. Put a line of adhesive around the perimeter of the strip and a broken bead down the center. Using a gentle back-and-forth motion, slide the strips into place. You can create straight, herringbone, and parquet patterns. Any excess adhesive can be peeled or cut away after it has dried. After drying, the strips can be stained and/or sealed if desired.

Wood Strip

Wood strip can be used as an alternative or supplement to traditional paneling. It can be used to create an accent wall or wainscoting as well as interesting designs and wall art. Each package of wood strip covers approximately 33 square feet of wall space. To determine the amount you will need, find the area of the wall and divide by 33. For example, 10 feet × 9 feet = 90 square feet; 90 ÷ 33 = 2.7 or approximately three packages of wood strip. This method will give you an adequate estimation for vertical and horizontal applications. Diagonal applications require 10 percent more material to allow for waste. Subtract the areas of doors, windows, and other openings that will not be covered.

Surface Preparation   Over rough surfaces such as plaster, light sanding should be sufficient to permit bonding. Wood strips can be directly applied to latex and acrylic surfaces, but enamel surfaces must be sanded. Adhesive will bond well to unfinished wood surfaces, but prefinished paneling is too slick. Rough it up by sanding. Vinyl wallcoverings should be stripped off. Paper ones can be left in place if they are in good condition. Just glue down any loose edges. It is not necessary to cover

Moldings

Wood moldings can work wonders on dull walls. They are inexpensive, versatile, readily available, and easy to use. They can be painted to blend or contrast or can be stained to match or accent the natural wood grain. They can be applied vertically, horizontally, diagonally, or in combination with wallcoverings. The versatility of wood molding can make a room traditional, contemporary, or anything you wish it to be. They are easy to cut, fit together, glue, nail, and finish. The moldings are also available in a wide variety of sizes and patterns.

There are a large number of stock wood and plastic moldings available at local home centers and lumberyards. Most moldings are usually used just around windows and doors, and at the juncture of floor or ceiling. By using your imagination, however, the decorating possibilities using molding are almost endless.

Mitered joints are sometimes required to create certain effects. Mitering a molding usually means to cut the ends at 45-degree angles so the two pieces form a 90-degree corner. It is important to do this carefully so a good joint results. A miter box is nec-

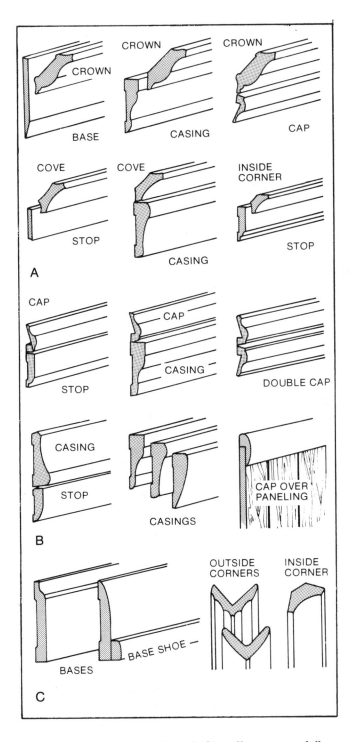

(A) Ceiling, (B) chair rail, and (C) wall corner and floor moldings.

It is sometimes necessary to cope moldings in order to get a tight fit at an inside corner. Coping means to cut the profile of the molding being butted up against the first piece. To cope a joint, first cut a 45-degree miter on the piece. It should be positioned in the miter box just as if the back of the miter box were the wall or whatever surface this piece is being put against. The resulting cut exposes the profile of the molding, serving as a template. Use the coping saw and cut along the profile made by the miter, holding the saw perpendicular to the piece. The result is a profile that fits tightly against the first piece.

The beauty of wood molding can only be enhanced by you and a finishing job well done. The techniques described for painting walls and finishing solid wood paneling can also be applied to unfinished wood moldings.

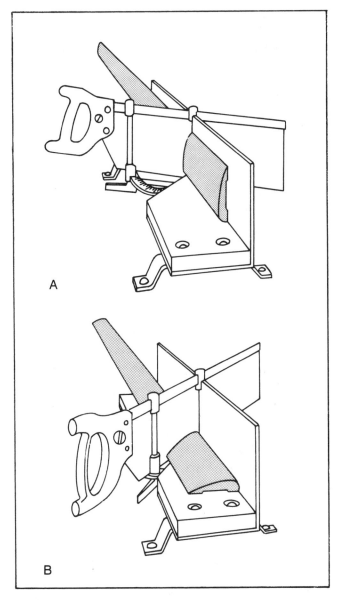

Mitering (A) baseboard, and (B) door and window molding.

essary since it has guides for the saw at a 45-degree angle. The molding is either placed flat on the bottom or against the back of the miter box depending on how the molding is to be used. It helps to clamp the molding in place when cutting, so it will not slip in the hand, resulting in an uneven cut.

To form a 90-degree corner, one 45-degree angle is cut from the left-hand side of the miter box and one from the right-hand side of the miter box.

Index